INNOVATION AGE LEARNING

Empowering Students by Empowering Teachers

SHARON "SAM" SAKAI-MILLER

International Society for Technology in Education
Eugene, Oregon • Arlington, Virginia

Innovation Age Learning
Empowering Students by Empowering Teachers
Sharon "Sam" Sakai-Miller

Editor: Emily Reed
Production Manager: Christine Longmuir
Copy Editor: Elizabeth Whipple
Proofreader: Ann Skaugset
Indexer: Wendy Allex
Book Design & Production: Kim McGovern

Library of Congress Cataloging-in-Publication Data

Sakai-Miller, Sharon, author.
   Innovation age learning : empowering students by empowering teachers / Sharon "Sam" Sakai-Miller.
      pages cm
   Includes bibliographical references and index.
   ISBN 978-1-56484-355-5 (pbk.) — ISBN 978-1-56484-495-8 (ebook)
   1. Critical thinking—Study and teaching. 2. Information literacy—Study and teaching. 3. Education—Effect of technological innovations on.
   4. Educational technology. 5. Information society.   I. Title.
   LB1590.3.S247 2015
   372.47'4—dc23
                                                      2015030256

First Edition
ISBN: 978-1-56484-355-5
Ebook version available.

Printed in the United States of America

About ISTE

The International Society for Technology in Education (ISTE) is the premier nonprofit organization serving educators and education leaders committed to empowering connected learners in a connected world. ISTE serves more than 100,000 education stakeholders throughout the world.

ISTE's innovative offerings include the ISTE Conference & Expo, one of the biggest, most comprehensive ed tech events in the world—as well as the widely adopted ISTE Standards for learning, teaching and leading in the digital age and a robust suite of professional learning resources, including webinars, online courses, consulting services for schools and districts, books, and peer-reviewed journals and publications. Visit iste.org to learn more.

Related ISTE Titles

Flip Your Classroom: Reach Every Student in Every Class Every Day, by Jonathan Bergmann and Aaron Sams

Active Learning: Reimagining Learning Spaces for Student Success, by Peggy Grant, Dale Basye, Stefanie Hausman, and Tod Johnston

About the Author

Sharon "Sam" Sakai-Miller is the director of Technology Integration Services (formerly known as Educational and Information Technology) at the San Lorenzo Unified School District, near Oakland, California. After teaching for 10 years, Sam focused her energies on furthering ed tech after witnessing how technology can enhance learning and teaching in dramatic ways.

Sam has served at three Bay Area County Offices of Education and as a curriculum coordinator for math, science, and instructional technology. As an educational consultant, she has presented in 18 states and published the MentorToGo Technology Literacy Kit for Teachers. Sam is a graduate of Pepperdine University's Online Master of Arts in Educational Technology and Doctoral Program for Educational Technology.

Acknowledgments

Writing this book has been a seven-year journey, so there are many people I must thank who helped along the way. I owe a debt of gratitude to the outstanding professors at Pepperdine University, where I conceived the idea for the book during my pursuit of advanced degrees in educational technology. Many thanks to Dr. Linda Polin for introducing me to Communities of Practice, cooperative learning, and Lateral Mentoring. I often relied on her wisdom to get through both the master of arts and doctoral programs. Dr. Farzin Majidi taught me that statistics could be enlightening and a "piece of pastry," depending on how you approached it. Most of all, I am grateful to my dissertation committee—to Dr. Paul Sparks for believing in me and chairing the committee, to Dr. Kay Davis for patiently but firmly holding me to a high standard, and to Dr. Ray Gen for giving me perspective and not giving up on me.

Special thanks to Kirk Brown, who worked alongside me to co-construct the instructional strategy of the dissertation study and generously shared his syllabus and other resources in the name of research.

I have had the good fortune to work with many dedicated professionals in the educational technology community who, like me, have had to weather budget cuts. Though their funding fluctuated, their moral support never did. Kudos to my friends at the County Offices of Education in Contra Costa, Alameda, Santa Clara, Marin, and Napa. I must also thank my friends at the regional California Technology Assistance Project (CTAP) offices for mentoring me and providing moral support. In particular, I want to acknowledge Dana Greenspan for taking me under her wing in the beginning and later encouraging me to write this book.

I must recognize the amazing staff at San Lorenzo Unified School District. I have been inspired by their creativity, desire to learn, and dedication. I work with a wonderful team of IT and ed tech professionals who could be making more money in industry but choose to work with students and teachers because they care. Thank you, Dr. Brill, for restructuring district leadership to bring both sides of the house together and to make technology integration a priority for all learners.

If it weren't for the awesome energy and inspiring atmosphere at the ISTE conference, this book would never have come to fruition. I just had to have one of those "ISTE Author" ribbons to add to the long trail that graced my nametag, so I engaged in conversation with Jeff Bolkan. Little did I know that the man with the gaudy red apron was the acquisitions editor! The job of asking hard questions and shepherding the project along lay in the very capable, inspiring hands of Lynda Gansel. I will be forever grateful for her belief in me and the guidance she afforded me as a rookie ISTE author. Kudos to Jodie Pozo-Olono for encouraging me to speak with courage and conviction and editor Emily Reed for artfully and astutely bringing this work to completion.

I am blessed to have the love and support of my parents, husband, and children. My dad always stood behind me and taught me to think, care, and value education—not just my own but that of all children and adults. My mom was always there with spiritual support and enthusiasm. My grown children, Shayna, James, and Scott, continue to motivate and challenge me to stay the course, be original, and keep up with new and exciting innovations. Finally, I could not have written this book or landed this job without the support and love of Dr. Mark Miller, superintendent of Juneau School District. Yes, I married my mentor.

Contents

PART I
Education in the Innovation Age

CHAPTER 1
Thriving in the Innovation Age

CHAPTER 2
Teaching at Three Levels: What, So What, and Now What

CHAPTER 3
Systemic Classroom Changes

PART II
Empowering Students through the 4Cs

PART III
Teachers' Innovation Age Challenge

Foreword

I begin many presentations with the reminder that we live and teach in a truly amazing time. It really is true. Even in our own short lifetimes, the world has been made smaller and larger at the same time. We can be connected to everything and everyone and the opportunity for deep and meaningful change and connections are ever-present. The past seven years in particular have seen the rise in social media platforms that have helped give everyone a voice and a seat at the table to share and learn.

In talking with educators from around the world at conferences and online, we often exchange stories of when the passion for teaching was re-sparked by learning something new. Often from behind a screen, and often from a stranger who would soon become a follower, ally, and friend as we journey on to being a better educator, teacher, and facilitator in and out of the classroom.

Despite living and teaching in this truly amazing time, it is not free from challenges. The role of the educator is made all the more difficult when what we feel we need to do for our students sits in sometimes direct conflict to what we are being asked to do. Upon examining this feeling more, it is often more gray and fuzzy in the sense that we all seem to know the outcomes or ideals we wish to strive toward, but without some concrete examples and road mapping it all seems out of reach in many ways.

A troubling dichotomy that has been exacerbated in the past five years or so has been the rift between the culture of learning and the culture of testing what has been learned. Ideas like the maker movement, coding in the classroom, and ways to bring more collaboration, creativity, communication, and critical-thinking into the classroom are oftentimes in stark contrast to initiatives that want to quantify all learning by way of a number two pencil. With so much focus being put on the outcome of an exam, we lose sight of what innovation and the spirit behind what we want for our students is all about. It is not about the success, it is truly about how and why we got to that point and then having the drive, grit, or enough spirit left to move beyond.

In *Innovation Age Learning: Empowering Students by Empowering Teachers,* Sam Sakai-Miller digs in deep and dissects many of the buzz-wordy phrases that permeate the educational culture. We all want innovative thinkers and makers, but this book explores actionable ideas and ways that students can reach their potential by helping teachers rethink the what and how of teaching and learning in the modern classroom.

Our students don't have to invent the next big thing. That's not the point or goal of innovative teaching. Students need to be given the challenge to create and share work that is meaningful to them and the world in which they live because it is possible. We need not to imbue with the ideas, but unlock their potential to think of new ideas, to dream, and then to act.

The beauty of this book is that it will take you on a quest to discover many ways that you can prepare the students you teach today for the world of tomorrow without losing sight of what matters in the present. It forgoes the crystal-ball pontification and replaces this with soundly researched and well laid out examples of how small changes to teaching can make profound differences to the learning outcomes. The changes are important and meaningful, and with this book you've started that journey to fostering the classroom today that will help all our children succeed.

—*Adam Bellow*

Dedication

This book is dedicated to all who dare to make a difference, starting with Miller, my children, my parents, my teachers, colleagues, and mentors. Together we're building for the future and keeping dreams alive.

Introduction

It was 2008 and I had just finished a two-week dissertation study entitled *Learning through Student-Authored Interactive Media: A Mixed Methods Exploration*. In the study, Advanced Biology students learned about mitosis, the cell cycle, and cancer by creating eModules that included tutorials and self-correcting tests. The average improvement on the post-study test was 547%. Twenty percent of the students who scored 20% or less on the pre-study test scored 80% or more on the post-study test. As we resolve to close the achievement gap, I thought these results were noteworthy.

In addition, student journals and surveys showed that building eModules was a positive experience, raising student awareness of metacognition, or what had helped them learn. I was eager to share this data with educators to show that technology has a vital role in the classroom. I wanted to arm every ed tech enthusiast with my results. I had co-constructed the instructional strategy with Milliken Award-winning teacher Kirk Brown in 2008. We based it on research on constructivism, constructivism and technology, and constructivism and biology. There were lots of teacher takeaways—and the basis for a viable, teacher-friendly book.

I know it is a cliché to say that timing is everything. In this case, timing *changed* everything.

When the dissertation study was conceived, the information age prevailed and No Child Left Behind and high-stakes testing made knowledge acquisition a priority. The internet was the information highway that led to all knowledge if you had the right search skills. The first iPhones had just hit the market. Facebook and Twitter were in their infancy. Crowd-sourcing and crowd-funding had yet to tap into the potential of ad hoc problem-solving. Information and data were drivers of change and success.

Jump ahead several years. Technology has amplified how we communicate, collaborate, and create: it has ushered in a new era, the Innovation Age. Information is now just a Google search away. We have info-glut. In the Innovation Age it is not about what you know, but what you do with what you know. To prepare our students to survive and thrive in the workplace, educators need to go beyond the information-age benchmarks of knowledge transfer and construction of meaning, and empower students to find solutions to unmet needs. These needs can be universal, for instance slowing global warming and the extinction of endangered animals, or ending hunger. They can be personal or local, like finding a way to keep hydrated at school or providing continuous wireless access for all students. Finding solutions for such needs requires understanding the problem, deciding on an acceptable solution, and determining the solution's feasibility. Why hasn't this need been met?

This book was written for teachers who directly impact students and can empower them with Innovation Age learning so they will survive and thrive in tomorrow's workplace. This book is also for those of you who want to better understand the challenges and needs facing today's learners and educators.

Part One compares learning and teaching in the Innovation Age and the information age, and why the experience should be different. Part Two focuses on how teachers can empower students through Innovation Age learning. It is packed with instructional takeaways from my dissertation study and research on innovation. Part Three is a call to action: teachers need to work together to ensure that all students benefit from Innovation Age learning.

While I was working on version six of this book, a friend called me a real "change agent." Me? I never fancied myself to be an agent of change. I just wanted to be a teacher and a tech mentor, and explore new tech frontiers. Being a change agent sounds daunting, but if that's what is required to empower teachers and the legion of others who support them to get technology into the hands of every student so they can contribute and compete in today's global society, I welcome the title. Become a change agent with me. We have to crowd-source a solution to make profound, rapid change in our classrooms. Our students are counting on us.

PART I

Education in the Innovation Age

What is most unique about the Innovation Age is the change in the role of innovation itself. To survive and maintain competitive advantage in the Innovation Age, [organizations] must continuously innovate.

—Tarak Modi, author of *Living in the Innovation Age*

Look around you. We are surrounded by evidence that we live in the Innovation Age. But we're teaching like it is still the information age. The first part of this book describes Innovation Age teaching and learning and outlines the changes we need to make to foster a new generation of innovators.

Chapter 1 Thriving in the Innovation Age

Information has never been more readily available. We have an abundance of smart devices, web-enabled mobile devices, and a variety of search engine options. Instead of information gathering, the emphasis is now on innovation and teamwork to discover new solutions and products. This chapter takes a top-level view of the Innovation Age, new demands on students, and implications for educators.

Chapter 2 Teaching at Three Levels: What, So What, and Now What

Think in terms of "What" (exposure), "So What" (engagement), and "Now What" (empowerment) to fully instill students with Innovation Age skills. Get beyond lower-order and higher-order thinking skills and embrace empathetic thinking skills.

Chapter 3 Systemic Classroom Changes

The effectiveness of nominal, unit-by-unit change is limited. Promoting Innovation Age learning requires broad systemic changes, such as creating a consistent learning environment, integrating technology systematically, and establishing iteration-friendly grading and assessment policies.

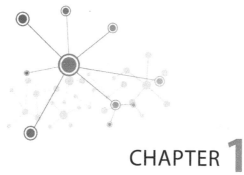

CHAPTER **1**

Thriving in the Innovation Age

We need to out-innovate, out-educate,
and out-build the rest of the world.

— President Barack Obama,
State of the Union Address, January 2011

Are we really in the Innovation Age? What demands does it place on students? How can educators prepare students to thrive in the Innovation Age? Instead of starting over, how can good instructional strategies be retrofitted to meet the needs of today's students?

What Do We Mean by "Innovation?"

The term "innovation" is used liberally when it comes to technology-infused initiatives, but it has several meanings. The *Merriam-Webster Online Dictionary* defines innovation as 1) the introduction of something new, or 2) a new idea, method, or device. Looking at the Latin origins, innovation means "to renew or change into new."

Innovation can easily be confused with creativity, invention, and improvement. It is important to understand the difference. Creativity is about the expression of or impetus behind ideas and thinking, while innovation is the implementation of an idea. Whereas invention is about the creation of a novel device, innovation is in the use of such ideas or methods. Improvement is doing the same thing better, while innovation may take an existing practice in a new direction.

Its scale can categorize innovation. Disruptive innovation is a radical change that starts at the bottom of a [market] system and relentlessly moves up to replace the existing leader (Zhao, 2012). Personal computers triggered disruptive innovation because they created a vast new market for accessible data. Craigslist changed the way classified ads are posted and viewed; iTunes drastically changed the way we acquire and listen to music.

Sustaining innovation is characterized by changes to an existing model and how it is used (Modi, 2011). Cell phone developers like to claim each new model is a sustaining innovation. Business leaders have identified different models of innovation that benefit their companies by rethinking internal processes and changing the way goods or services are provided. Amazon's Jeff Bezos, for one. Solar entrepreneurs offer an environmentally-friendly alternative that taps into existing power systems.

Innovation can take any form; it has prevailed for centuries. So why are we suddenly in the Innovation Age?

The Information Age
Gives Way to the Innovation Age

In the information age, the use of computer technology and the internet made it possible to collect and disseminate information in digital form. The dominant economic force shifted from manufacturing to creating systems that could efficiently access, generate, and analyze data, turn it into information, and consolidate the content into accessible knowledge. Information such as books, images, music, and periodicals became readily available online. Students with access to the internet were taught information literacy and digital-age skills; those who couldn't attend certain classes often enrolled in online courses.

The Innovation Age can be seen as a response to "info-glut" and the tech-savvy, globally connected economy brought about by information-age advances. We live in a time where success has become less about knowledge and more about what one does with it. Continuous improvement and innovation is the responsibility of all workers, not just the research and development department. Companies of all sizes train their members to be effective collaborators, communicators, creators, and critical thinkers.

Here are some indicators that innovation, not pure information, rules the day:

- Would you rather invest in a start-up or a bookstore?

- Would students prefer a Maker Faire or a trivia contest?

- Should students simply show their results, or show multiple ways of solving the problem?

- Would you rather "Ask an Expert" or "crowd-source" a solution?

Organizations, including those in education, can no longer justify the this-is-the-curriculum-I have-always-used mindset. Instead, they must incorporate collaboration, communication, creativity, and critical thinking and rely less on multiple-choice tests and single "right" answers.

To be competitive in the global economy, every nation needs to develop future innovators. In order to meet this challenge, we need to first understand how successful innovators work.

Innovation Process

One thing innovators have in common is that they enjoy collaborative work. The innovation process generally starts with a problem and involves an idea or solution, multiple perspectives, revision, and persistence. Let's look at the steps in the innovation process as described by two innovation experts, David Kelley and Tarak Modi.

David Kelley, founder of IDEO, an international design and consulting firm located in Palo Alto, California, has been in the innovation business for decades. His company has been credited with designing more than 1,000 products, but he is perhaps most famous for working with Steve Jobs.

Kelley also founded the Hasso Plattner Institute of Design (d.school) at Stanford University. Graduate students from different disciplines participate in this program, which encourages innovation in terms of design thinking, or thinking like a designer. The program doesn't lead to a certificate or degree and still the number of applicants is far greater than the number of spots available.

In a 2013 episode of *60 Minutes,* Kelley said, "The big thing about design thinking is it allows people to build on the ideas of others. Instead of just having this one thread…we get to a place that we could not have reached on our own. You have to have diversity and collaboration…empathy for the consumer." He advocates identifying the big idea and looking to others to generate exciting ideas. Kelley's primary steps for design thinking:

1. **Inspiration.** Go into the field to gain a better understanding of your user and their challenge, whether it is in their domain or unrelated domains.

2. **Synthesis.** Make sense of your findings by looking for patterns.

3. **Ideation and Experimentation.** Consider all options and experiment with numerous prototypes, without becoming attached to any one solution. Get feedback from multiple stakeholders and hear all perspectives.

4. **Implementation.** Refine the "best" solution and roll it out.

There is no magic formula for innovation. Tarak Modi is an innovation expert and author of many articles on its process. In his book *Living in the Innovation Age:*

Five Principles for Prospering in the New Era (2011), Modi describes six phases in what he calls the "Innovation Life Cycle":

1. **Ideation.** Ideas are submitted, discussed, and rated.

2. **Selection.** The "best" ideas are selected and moved into the process.

3. **Inception.** Selected ideas are developed to a high degree of detail.

4. **Presentation.** Selected ideas are presented to stakeholders.

5. **Elaboration.** Stakeholder-selected projects are mapped out against projected milestones/goals and timeline.

6. **Transition.** Implementation of product, prototype, or demonstration of innovation.

While the six phases of the Innovation Life Cycle apply to business development, there are two important takeaways for educators: 1) the innovation process is fluid and iterative, and 2) its adoption cycle no longer takes years. Companies that have a protracted adoption cycle risk losing their competitive edge. Likewise, education needs to keep innovating for students to remain competitive.

Traits of Successful Innovators

Is the ability to innovate determined by nurture or nature?

Researchers have estimated that roughly two-thirds of our innovation skills can be learned or nurtured. In *The Innovator's DNA: Mastering the Five Skills of Disruptive Innovators* (2011), authors Dyer, Gregersen, and Christensen identify five skills that underpin the ability to innovate: questioning, observing, networking, experimenting, and associational thinking.

In *Creating Innovators: The Making of Young People Who Will Change the World* (2012), Tony Wagner lists the essential qualities of successful innovators as curiosity, collaboration (which begins with listening and learning from other perspectives), associational or integrative thinking, and bias toward action and experimentation. He also says that these qualities are not limited to those born predisposed to innovation, but can and should be encouraged in all learners through a process that includes play, leads to passion, and matures into purpose.

New Demands on Students

Students who understand the innovation process and develop traits that successful innovators possess will have a distinct advantage when they enter the work force. Because skillsets needed for success in the Innovation Age are not as clear-cut as they were in the information age we must incorporate the ability to handle ambiguity and change into education. According to a 1999 U.S. Department of Labor report entitled *Future Work Trends and Challenges for Work in the 21st Century,* 65% of today's grade school kids will end up at a job that has yet to be invented. Skeptics have challenged the validity of the 65% figure and called it "teacher myth," but Google had not been invented by the time any of the 11,333 employees at the Mountain View, CA headquarters were out of grade school (The Verge, 2014). Many innovative companies such as Facebook, Amazon, Twitter, and Instagram did not exist when their current employees were in grade school.

Students who grow up in a high-tech age and global economy will face a more complex world. Whether students pursue careers in retail, research, or racing, the problems they tackle will be more complex. For instance, 50 years ago a coffee shop could use manual cash registers, but businesses today require computerized registers, credit card readers, and other forms of digital currency. Digital sales require security, programming, and computerized recordkeeping. Cancer researchers have access to far more data, precision tools, sophisticated techniques, and pharmaceutical compounds than ever. A racecar driver has far more to contend with than the course; they must understand more complicated cars, security and safety measures, and social media.

In order to thrive in a more complicated world, students will need to understand how to work collaboratively with collective intelligence. Collaboration necessitates communication. Solutions require tenacity, creativity, and critical thinking. While students need to possess core knowledge and skills, they must be adroit with technology and prepared for the demands of the Innovation Age.

Students can no longer be content with finding the right answer because the questions are constantly changing. Consider the classic word problem: how long will it take a driver traveling at a constant speed of 60 miles an hour to complete a 600-mile journey? The correct mathematical answer would be 10 hours. A more useful answer could be found using Google maps because one could find current or predicted traffic conditions, alternate routes, and rest, gas, and food stops along the way because the driver could not make a 10-hour drive without stopping. Embracing ambiguity is one of author Michael J. Gelb's seven steps to thinking like Leonardo da Vinci (Gelb, 2000). Instead of focusing on the right answer, he directs us to seek the right questions.

Students need to observe how they learn because the Innovation Age demands lifelong learning and finding solutions to unmet needs. They need to be able to research new or related topics that emerge during the fluid innovation process. In the iterative solution development process, they must be able to adapt to the unexpected, such as user feedback from multiple perspectives, product failures, unforeseen market conditions, and competing solutions. Students must develop metacognition—cognition about cognition—as they learn core knowledge and skills.

Makers, Coders, Inventers, Entrepreneurs, Authors

Some students are already answering the call to innovate. 2014 Google Science Fair winner Ann Makosinski created a flashlight that works off the power generated from the palm of the human hand so students without electricity could study at night. 2013 Intel Science Talent Search winner Sara Volz won $100,000 for her research on algae as an alternate fuel source. She built her lab under her loft bed. 2014 Nobel Peace Prize winner and Palestine activist Malala Yousafzai has been working courageously for the right to education for all children, especially girls.

What makers, gamers, coders, inventors, entrepreneurs, and student authors have in common is that they are "prosumers"—they produce something of value while consuming information. They are not passively acquiring knowledge and proving mastery solely through summative content-based assessments.

Makers

In the March 17, 2014 edition of *Adweek,* Joan Voight defined the "maker movement" as:

> ...the umbrella term for independent inventors, designers and tinkerers. A convergence of computer hackers and traditional artisans, the niche is established enough to have its own magazine, *Make,* as well as hands-on Maker Faires that are catnip for DIYers who used to toil in solitude. Makers tap into an American

admiration for self-reliance and combine that with open-source learning, contemporary design and powerful personal technology, like 3-D printers. The creations, born in cluttered local workshops and bedroom offices, stir the imaginations of consumers numbed by generic, mass-produced, made-in–China merchandise.

The pendulum is swinging the other way. In a time where many schools have dropped home economics, shop, and arts and crafts, people are turning away from mass-produced goods in favor of unique products made by individuals. New technologies have made it possible for makers to market their wares—eBay and Etsy connect millions of buyers with sellers. Paypal and BitCoin have increased payment options that were once limited to merchants.

Maker Faires are becoming increasingly popular as lifelong learners of all ages gather and participate in viewing and testing self-made products. The White House hosted its first Maker Faire in June of 2014 to "encourage a new generation of makers and manufacturers to share their talents and hone their skills (www.whitehouse.gov/nation-of-makers)." Maker Faires are held across the U.S. and in countries such as Africa, Japan, and the UK.

Students learn by making. A 2014 article in *Edutopia* magazine advocated encouraging teachers to be makers themselves. In the article, "Supporting the Teacher Maker Movement," author Heather Wolpert-Gawron suggests that teacher makers will in turn bring this rich learning experience to their students.

Coders

Whether they are writing code, or cracking it, students are mastering vital digital-age skills, honing their problem-solving skills, and finding subjects like math more interesting through coding. Students of all ages can write code using a number of applications and apps. MIT Labs' Scratch (http://scratch.mit.edu) has been free of charge for many years, and students use it to create games, animations, and stories. Tynker (www.tynker.com) is a free web-based app that teaches students to code at their own pace. Codecademy (www.codecademy.com) offers free interactive courses on programming in Python, JavaScript, PHP, Ruby, and HTML.

The opportunities coding affords students are many. In 2014, the San Lorenzo Unified School District partnered with the REACH Youth Center and County Office to run a "hack-a-thon," where students competed to create the best app to solve a health issue. At this event, coding apps were the mediating tool for constructivist learning about the health issue, local resources, and coding. Students were fully immersed in an innovative learning environment where they collaborated, researched, experimented, problem-solved, questioned, and used creative thinking. Teams also competed for prizes.

Cracking code involves deciphering code written by others. In this digital world where encryption and data security are so critical, students need exposure to code at an early age. One interesting program is CryptoClub (www.cryptoclub.org). Created by Janet Beissinger and Bonnie Saunders of the Learning Sciences Research Institute at the University of Illinois, the program teaches cyphering and middle school math concurrently. In this instance, students develop problem-solving skills by decoding cyphers and applying math concepts. The creators of code.org (http://code.org) believe every student should have the opportunity to learn computer science; they offer anyone an introductory First Hour of Code, as well as teaching and learning resources.

The terms "programming" and "coding" are often, and erroneously, used interchangeably. Coding, which is the language of programmers, has gained popularity and visibility with actions such as First Hour of Code. Like any language, coding needs to be practiced regularly to build fluency. Creating special events, code days or code weeks, offers gateways for exposing students to coding and to apps like Hopscotch, Daisy the Dinosaur, Tynker, Scratch, Scratch Jr., and Lightbot Programming Puzzles.

Entrepreneurs

Entrepreneurship is "the undertaking of significant new projects or activities through management, organization, and assumption of the risks," according to Yong Zhao (2012), a leading authority on how globalization and technology impact education. He advocates taking project-based learning a step further by providing opportunities for students to produce marketable products. The concept is almost an amalgamation of the Maker Movement, project-based learning, constructivism, and Innovation Age learning. Zhao believes that students will be more intrinsically motivated to produce something of greater quality if the result is marketable (2012). This experience will engage students in skills they will need for jobs that do not currently exist. In fact, Zhao goes so far as to say that:

forcing children to master the same curriculum essentially discrimi-
nates against talents that are not consistent with the prescribed
knowledge and skills. Students who are otherwise talented but do
not do well in the prescribed subjects are often sent to spend more
time on the core subjects, retained for another grade, or deprived of
the opportunity to develop their talents in other ways. (p. 45)

Students should learn to take ownership of their learning and set high standards
for their projects (and products), but educators should not abandon the concept of
core content. In the Innovation Age, educators need to be flexible so that students
have a variety of innovative approaches or learning opportunities to put their ideas
into action. In addition to knowing how important it is to understand how they
learn (metacognition), students should also have a firm grasp of the innovation
cycle so they can develop their entrepreneurship.

Student Authors of Curriculum

The idea of students writing and marketing curriculum is intriguing. The benefits
for student authors are obvious: they develop deep content knowledge and
strengthen their communication, collaboration, creativity, and critical thinking
skills. By creating works that matter to them, students also want to produce
higher-quality projects and explore opportunities to self-publish—podcasts,
YouTube, and peer-editing sites. If they are enterprising they can learn business
skills as well.

The next chapter describes how students from Tracy High School created interactive curriculum modules to learn about mitosis, the cell cycle, and cancer as part
of a dissertation study, *Learning through Student-Authored Interactive Media*. Due to
the course's pacing limitations, the students did not have enough time to polish,
publish, and market their curriculum eModules. As educators explore involving
students in the development of curriculum, they will also have to consider
building more time into the schedule to allow students to publish their work.

New Demands on Education

If innovation is the new normal, is education embracing it and rising to its challenge? The demands of the Innovation Age on educational organizations are two-fold: they must be innovative to remain viable and solvent, and they need to adapt their instructional content to prepare students to thrive in the Innovation Age.

Viable Educational Organizations

Public schools and districts, private schools, public and private charter schools, virtual schools, and home schools all compete for limited educational dollars. There is constant pressure on public education to reduce waste, eliminate bureaucracy, streamline policy, and do more with less. The public and media are in essence calling for business-model innovation that will improve the way goods and services are provided.

If we want students to value innovation, we as educators must show an appreciation for it. We need to "walk the talk" and demonstrate a desire to be innovative, fresh, and flexible in how we address the unmet needs of our students. Leveraging innovative, tech-infused curricula is one way we show the community that we value innovation. We need to exhibit an innovation mindset that permeates every classroom, hall, staff room, and office.

The Obama administration implemented high-stakes competitive grant programs, such as Race-to-the-Top and Investing in Innovation (i3) to spur innovation in the educational system. Our current system of defining student achievement—based on performance on standardized tests—dampens creativity, innovation, and entrepreneurship.

For the U.S. to be competitive in the new global economy, we need to "develop the creative and enterprising capacities of all our students" (Wagner, 2012) so we can, per President Obama, "out-innovate, out-educate, and out-build the rest of the world" (2011). Business and political leaders urge innovation in the fields of science, technology, engineering, and mathematics (STEM). They assert that the economic future of our country depends on strong STEM education (U.S. Department of Education, 2011). Is the call for innovative curriculum or innovation curriculum? The answer is both.

Supporting Future Innovators

Educational organizations have to support innovation in an intentional, not incidental, manner or their students will be at a distinct disadvantage. The iterative, collaborative, and rapidly morphing processes of the Innovation Age are in stark contrast to educational practices that have been in place for some time. In short order, educators need to adopt content that supports the 4Cs of the Common Core State Standards (collaboration, communication, creativity, and critical thinking), encourage traits that help innovators succeed, and establish curriculum that reinforces the importance of innovation.

In the Innovation Age, educators must expect to teach beyond exposure to basic content and engage student innovators to contribute new ideas or solutions to unmet needs. Their "floor" is a mastery of basic concepts and skills, regular attendance, and active classroom participation. They must take their core knowledge and ask what it empowers them to do. In other words, students must be encouraged to continue using their empathetic thinking skills and honor multiple perspectives in any context.

In order to take instructional strategies to the next level, educators themselves need to be familiar with the innovation process, the traits of successful innovators, and ways to infuse these traits into current instructional strategies, such as constructivism.

Benchmarks and Standards

Economic drivers of each new age have determined the primary goals of education. To implement these goals, new objectives are identified, which in turn produce changes in strategies and activities. The success of those changes can be measured and evaluated.

Think big picture. What is the educational imperative of the Innovation Age? If everyone is responsible for their own growth and self-improvement, then the overarching goal of the era is to empower all students to innovate and find solutions to unmet needs.

We can better understand the demands of the Innovation Age and its implications for education by comparing key economic drivers, workforce development methods, and educational imperatives and benchmarks. Doing so, we see how the skills and demands of each new age build upon the previous ages. For example, workers in the Innovation Age can produce goods and services (industrial age) and access and organize data (information age) while designing solutions to unmet needs (Innovation Age). Table 1.1 compares the economic drivers for the industrial age, information age, and Innovation Age and their impact on education.

Table 1.1 | Economic Drivers and Education in the Industrial, Information, and Innovation Ages

	Industrial Age	Information Age	Innovation Age
Key Economic Drivers	Production of goods and services	Improving access to information and data	Designing solutions to unmet needs
Workforce Development Methods	Training as needed	Theme-based face-to-face and online workshops	Face-to-face and virtual collaboration, research and crowd-sourcing
Educational Imperative	Literacy	Knowledge creation	Innovation
Educational Benchmarks	Reading, writing, arithmetic	Reading, writing, arithmetic Content knowledge, research, information communication technology (ICT)	Reading, writing, arithmetic Content knowledge, research, information communication technology (ICT) Collaboration, communication, creativity, and critical thinking (4Cs)

The educational benchmarks have been additive. When the focus was literacy, students needed reading, writing, and basic math skills. As the educational imperative expanded during the information age, content knowledge, ability to research, and technology literacy were added to the expectations of high school graduates. With advances in technology and today's global market, high school graduates need to also be able to collaborate, communicate effectively, be creative, and think critically.

Although the benchmarks have been additive, instructional minutes have not. But that is a good thing. An integrated, project-based approach has shown to be a more engaging way to address basic skills, content knowledge, and technology literacy. Teachers are just starting to implement the Common Core and the 4Cs so there is not much data on how effectively they are being incorporated with the other benchmarks.

Traits of Successful Innovators and the 4Cs

Nurturing successful innovators starts by understanding the traits that are part of their DNA and incorporating them into current educational standards. Examine the traits of successful innovators vis-à-vis the 4Cs in Table 1.2. Which traits support which skills? Draw lines to connect them.

Table 1.2 | Innovation Skills and the 4Cs

Innovation Skills	4Cs
Questioning	Collaboration
Observing	Communication
Networking	Creativity
Experimenting	Critical Thinking
Associational Thinking	

Arguably, any and every trait or innovation skill can be paired with another. Some combinations include:

- Questioning during the revision process enhances critical thinking

- Questioning to assess needs enhances communication

- Observing is part of communication or the fact-finding aspect of critical thinking

- Networking can be a product of collaboration or good communication

- Experimenting is part of the creative process or critical thinking

- Associational thinking enhances creativity and critical thinking

Table 1.3 demonstrates how the skills are combined, which will be further explored in Part Two of this book. Listing and defending all of the possible connections in this book would soon become tedious. This exercise in associational thinking is better suited for personal and small-group discussion—it brings up many options and stimulates brainstorming. The key point is teacher awareness of the 4Cs and how to build them into their lessons. When students recognize innovation skills, they are able to consciously sharpen their aptitude for innovation. Because these skills can overlap and appear in many ways, teachers can consider the skills as multiple opportunities to reinforce innovative activity.

Table 1.3 | Connections between Innovation Skills and the 4Cs

Innovation Skills	4Cs
Questioning	Collaboration
Observing	Communication
Networking	Creativity
Experimenting	Critical Thinking
Associational Thinking	

Innovation Curriculum

If we are going to build student awareness for innovation, it must be integrated throughout the subjects. If we want students to go beyond being consumers of Innovation Age products, we need to give them opportunities to participate in the process.

There are calls for curricular innovation. Innovation has become a subject of study in business workshops, trainings, seminars, and online courses. These programs offer insights into research, "best practices," Modi's Innovation Life Cycle, and building innovation teams. Prominent colleges and universities such as Stanford, Wharton, and MIT offer programs that focus on innovation. Training manuals, such as ATD's *Innovation Training* (Hattori & Wycoff, 2004) and *Thomson Innovation Training*, provide further ideas. For K–12 teachers who want to foster innovation, The Henry Ford Museum has made Innovation 101 lesson modules and interactive curricula available online, through Creative Commons licensing at www.OnInnovation.org.

Innovation is not only a unit of study, but a forward-looking, problem-solving part of any class. It can be a natural extension of social studies, when students study inventors. They will note how crucial innovation is to science and engineering. Implementing innovations cannot occur without developing effective communication skills. Innovation can be embedded in technology electives. Holding a culminating "Innovation Fair" may be a way of including cross-curricular participation, and making innovation a quasi-team sport. Another idea is to offer innovation clubs as enrichment programs. The opportunities for incorporating and encouraging innovation are limited only by our imagination. It is not about adding one more thing to the curriculum; it is about adding relevance and currency to what we teach.

Summary

What   Based on research and anecdotal evidence, we are transitioning from the information age to the Innovation Age.

So What   For our students to survive and thrive in the Innovation Age, we need to help them develop Innovation Age skills as well as basic content knowledge and digital-age skills.

Now What Educators will examine successful information-age instructional strategies and enhance them with Innovation Age skills to empower students to become creative innovators, collaborators, communicators, and critical thinkers.

Up next …

Teaching at Three Levels: What, So What, Now What

Deepen student engagement and inclination to innovate by clarifying the learning outcomes as core concepts or skills, exploring their relevance and application, and making it a habit to use fresh knowledge in new ways or to find solutions to unmet needs.

CHAPTER 2

Teaching at Three Levels: What, So What, and Now What

Learning and innovation go hand in hand.
The arrogance of success is to think that what you
did yesterday will be sufficient for tomorrow.

— William Pollard, 19th-century clergyman

Now that information is readily available on the internet, there is less need to remember as much. Videos and online tutorials can deepen understanding on any topic and offer multiple applications. Armed with these resources, students are ready to engage with what they learn and able to use that knowledge in new and innovative ways. In the Innovation Age, teachers must find ways to empower students to take what they learn and challenge themselves to do something with it.

In February 2007, 51 advanced biology students from Tracy High School in Tracy, California worked in teams to create eModules (self-correcting tutorials) to learn about mitosis, the cell cycle, and cancer. During the two-week unit of study students created concept maps using Inspiration software, exported them as PowerPoint slideshows to enhance tutorial and quiz elements, and imported them into Adobe Captivate to make the finished eModules interactive. Each student reflected daily to four question prompts: What was your goal today? What did you accomplish today? What strategies worked well? What obstacles did you encounter?

After preparing the necessary technology, assessment, and curriculum resources, the teacher served as a "guide on the side" and provided only 10 minutes of direct instruction (because students had no idea what concept maps were or how to use Inspiration software).

When pre- and posttest scores were compared after the unit was over, the average gain was 547%, with 20% of the students improving from 20% or below to 80% or above. Student journals and exit surveys revealed that most students enjoyed the unit, benefitted from the use of technology and working in teams, and found that repeated exposure to the content while creating and debugging their eModules helped them better understand the subject.

The information-age goals of the unit were to learn about mitosis, the cell cycle, and cancer, explore how concepts in the unit were related to each other, and create eModules that would help other students master the unit of study. Incidentally, the students used Innovation Age skills to meet the learning goals. This leads to the question: How could this unit be improved by Innovation Age teaching?

Innovation Age skills—collaboration, questioning, and metacognition—should be identified and intentionally encouraged. As an ongoing part of Innovation Age learning, students would boost their "innovation DNA" by consciously working on their networking, observation, experimentation, questioning, and associational thinking skills. They would be conscious of the role the 4Cs played in their ability to complete their project at a high level.

Most importantly, students would be looking for how they could use what they know to find solutions to unmet needs. This questioning need not be restricted to the development of the eModule, instead encouraging students to use what they learned about mitosis, the cell cycle, and cancer to think open-endedly about solutions (new methods of treatment or ideas for a cure).

Exposure, Engagement, Empowerment

Innovation Age teaching elicits learning at three levels: exposure (what), engagement (so what), and empowerment (now what).

These levels of teaching refer to learning objectives, not a sequence of lessons. The demands of the Innovation Age call for teaching for empowerment—so students are taught to be solution seekers, not collectors of knowledge. Student engagement and activity should lead to empowerment instead of being the ultimate objective. Asking what, so what, and now what is vital to making learning relevant beyond school and good grades. The objective speaks to empowerment in the future: *Now what can you do with what you learned?* One possible answer for the students in the study was that—having deeper understanding of cancer by learning about mitosis and the cell cycle—they would be inspired to join the fight against cancer as researchers, caregivers or supports, or, perish the thought, brave patients.

Table 2.1 compares objectives, learning outcomes, thinking skills, and examples from the dissertation study for each of the three levels.

Table 2.1 | Three Levels Demonstrated by Dissertation Study

	What...	So What...	Now What...
Objective	Exposure	Engagement	Empowerment
Dual Learning Outcomes	Content knowledge, basic skills, literacy	Constructing meaning through active learning	Metacognition—learning how to learn
	Awareness of technology tools	Technology integration	Innovation—finding solutions to unmet needs
Thinking Skills	Lower-order thinking skills: • Remembering • Understanding • Applying content knowledge	Lower-order and higher-order thinking skills: • Analysis, • Evaluation, and • Creation/creativity	Lower-order, higher-order, and empathetic thinking skills: • Understanding user • Understanding problems • Designing a solution from multiple perspectives

Table continued from previous page

	What...	So What...	Now What...
Example: Dissertation Study	**IB Biology** Students will be able to: • Outline the stages in the cell cycle, including interphase (G1, S, G2), mitosis and cytokinesis. • Explain that tumors (cancers) are the result of uncontrolled cell division and that these can occur in any organ or tissue. • Explain that interphase is an active period in the life of a cell when many metabolic reactions occur, including protein synthesis, DNA replication and an increase in the number of mitochondria and/or chloroplasts. • Describe the events that occur in the four phases of mitosis (prophase, metaphase, anaphase, telophase). • Explain how mitosis produces two genetically identical nuclei. • State that growth, embryonic development, tissue repair and asexual reproduction involve mitosis.	**Technology** Students will be able to: • Brainstorm the stages of mitosis and cell cycle into steps and categories using Inspiration. • Convert an outline to a PPT document. • Use this as a basis to begin Adobe Captivate. • Produce an eLearning module using Adobe Captivate. • Deploy it and have others use it.	**Metacognition** Students will be able to: • Enhance learning (metacognition) • Document process • Ensure team accountability • Learning journal entries should include 1) daily goal, 2) what was accomplished, 3) what strategies worked well, and 4) what obstacles were encountered.

Mapping Content Standards to Innovation Age Skills

Thinking in terms of what, so what, and now what is easily incorporated in the planning stage and can be included in the setup of each lesson or unit. A simple recipe for mapping content standards against Innovation Age skills would include these steps:

Step 1	**Assemble Ingredients (What)**
	Examine the content standards and create a timeline for addressing them. (Your district may have a pre-mix for that.) Examine the grade-appropriate digital-age skills and create a sequence for introducing them. (See ISTE Standards for Students and/or local matrices of grade-appropriate technology skills.)
Step 2	**Mix and Match (So What)**
	Before you mix the two sets of ingredients, see how their sequences line up. Stir digital-age skills into content. Pepper with innovation skills throughout the mix.
Step 3	**Personalize (Now What)**
	Enjoin your students to use their learning to resolve unmet needs.

Empowerment inspires involvement and gives meaning to attaining foundational knowledge and skills. Engagement leads to deeper understanding of content knowledge and prepares a path to empowerment. School is relevant because it leads to empowerment and connects students to each other, to resources, and to the future. In other words, the work they do in class is not just for good grades.

Students look for personal relevance in the content and skills they learn, and consider themselves solution seekers. Educators cultivate this attitude by teaching students to collaborate, communicate, create, and think critically. In the process they build awareness for and ability to network, observe, question, experiment, and think associationally.

What: Exposure

Exposure to a solid core of content knowledge and skills is part of being educated. However, exposure to content is not the first step in the learning process—it is a component of learning for empowerment. Mastery of basics should not keep students from engaging in project-based learning, yet many students are relegated to drill-and-kill skill builders until they are deemed ready for projects. This is not just discouraging and demeaning; it keeps students from fully engaging in learning activities. In kid terms, school becomes boring when they can't get to the good stuff.

Lower-Order Thinking Skills

When teachers give equal weight to too many topics they will only have time to help students remember, understand, and apply key concepts for a limited time. The Common Core State Standards (CCSS) have fewer topics to allow teachers to explore them more deeply and to integrate digital age skills.

Remembering, understanding, and applying information are the three lower-order thinking skills in Bloom's taxonomy. When students are limited to "what" or to the exposure level, they tend to forget the content after the test.

Learning Outcomes

Zeroing in on "what" in terms of technology learning outcomes highlights the importance of technology skills and allows teachers to plan for broad coverage of technology skills instead of relying on an isolated computer class in middle or high school.

On its website, Brigham Young University defines learning outcomes for students as "statements that describe the knowledge, skills, and attitudes that learners should have after successfully completing a learning experience or program (BYU, 2006)." Some curriculum design guides use the terms "learning outcomes" and "standards" synonymously. The CCSS maps out grade-appropriate content standards for the respective disciplines from kindergarten through high school. This fosters greater consistency between states so students receive well-rounded instruction and avoid repeating topics at the expense of new ones, regardless of location. States that have not adopted CCSS have their own system of standards. The general practice in education is to unpack the standards and state them in terms that raise student learning outcomes.

"Wallpaper outcomes" are used only to introduce the unit, but have little or nothing to do with it (Wiliam, 2011). Conversely, "invisible outcomes" that are integral to the unit of study go without mention. If vital skills related to technology, innovation, collaboration, information fluency, critical thinking, and citizenship remain invisible or unstated, they will most likely go unassessed. Areas that are not graded or assessed lose importance and tend to fall by the wayside, especially for grade-conscious students.

Stating the content standards as student learning outcomes serves two purposes: it focuses the teacher on the incremental concepts and skills that students need to master, and focuses the students on what they need to accomplish and its relevance to them. The brain ascertains meaning before it will attend to details (Medina, 2008, p. 90). Digital-age skills need to be included in the "big picture" instead of being infused as "invisible outcomes" for students to deem them relevant or meaningful.

In the dissertation study, teacher Kirk Brown established dual learning outcomes on his syllabus. (See Table 2.1 for examples.) By listing two sets of outcomes—one content-based and one technology-related—the teacher legitimizes the use of technology tools and sets the parameters for how technology assets will be assessed.

Articulating dual learning standards leads to increasingly complex levels of technology use throughout students' academic careers. Generally speaking, students are assigned the same presentational reports, slide shows, and videos with a limited scope of communication challenges. If we mapped technology skills against content standards we would build in the expectation that these essential skills would be addressed in a progressively more sophisticated manner. At the very least, we would ensure a broader repertoire of communication and technology skills for students.

Standards and Expectations

No matter where you teach, content standards are readily accessible, often in multiple formats. You should map out the sequence and pacing of the standards at the start of the year if your district or grade level or subject matter team has not already done so.

Age-appropriate technology standards for students are also available. Most districts refer to the International Society for Technology in Education's standards (ISTE Standards) for Students for guidance. (ISTE standards for students, teachers, administrators, coaches, and computer science educators are available online at http://iste.org/standards.) Several states, counties, and districts have created a matrix for integrating technology skills into the CCSS by grade level. To see what the Fresno County Office of Education in California put together, visit http://commoncore.fcoe.org/subject/technology.

Chunking and Pairing

Too often teachers have to be concerned with simply providing access to technology or scheduling lab time to complete the obligatory tech-infused project. Pairing content with technology projects should be done very deliberately. At the beginning of the year, curriculum content is chunked into units of study and grade-appropriate technology projects are determined by access to computing devices. In the dissertation study, teacher Kirk Brown felt that this small unit would be ideal for peer teaching. The study took place in February, which gave him time to assign other PowerPoint projects and group work ahead of time. Brown felt that students would be able to pick up the concept map software (Inspiration) and the self-correcting quiz features of Adobe Captivate without extending the unit appreciably.

Similarly, teachers chunk the curriculum into units of study before the school year starts. If teachers consider age-appropriate technology projects for their students and map them in a continuum of complexity, they could strategically pair content with technology projects. Because technology tools are ubiquitous in all disciplines of study and careers, deliberate pairings would ensure that students have broad exposure to and proficiency with technology tools. In other words, if teachers take the same careful approach toward accruing technology skills, students will develop their technology-infused projects more efficiently.

Identifying Dual Learning Outcomes

Once the content and technology skills have been paired, it is important to articulate both sets of learning outcomes. When only the content standards are identified, the project work—which leads to deeper learning—is often seen as extraneous or time-consuming busywork.

The same is true about the other Innovation Age skills. Unless those "invisible outcomes" are stated and valued, they will not be developed. Students may use technology in and out of school, but are they building the skills to become technology producers instead of heavy consumers of technology? How can you build awareness for and develop the innovation skills of networking, observing, associational thinking, questioning, and experimenting if they are not even identified as desirable outcomes?

So What: Engagement

Innovative educators are inventive in how they seek to engage students in active learning. But activity doesn't always mean engagement, and engagement may not lead to empowerment.

Answers to the question "so what?" lead to meaning, relevance, and connectedness. What activities will provide deeper understanding and meaning to basic concepts and skills? Why is this topic relevant? How is this information connected to what was learned before or what is yet to be learned?

Constructivism is a study of knowledge that involves triggering students' curiosity to investigate and learn more about a topic. It hinges on the concept of construction of knowledge as opposed to replication of knowledge. The approach has influenced countless educators who aspire to empower students through active learning and demonstrating their knowledge through a variety of presentations (Jonassen, 2006; Juniu, 2006). The tenets of constructivism include these concepts:

- Meaning is constructed and personal

- Learning is socio-cultural

- Learning is based on the cognitive development of the learner

- Learning requires active engagement by the learner and is therefore learner-centered

- Mediating tools are needed to construct meaning

Higher-Order Thinking Skills

Constructivism is an instructional construct that encourages using higher-order thinking skills to personalize learning and take it to the "so what" level. Problem-based learning, which is based in constructivism, challenges the learner's involvement.

Analyzing, evaluating, and creating are the three higher-order thinking skills in Bloom's taxonomy. These align with the constructivist perspective that learners "learn from doing" to accommodate new information and assimilate it into their current conceptual framework (Dori & Belcher, 2005). As students create representations of what they've learned they must analyze and evaluate the information. When students engage in constructing representations of their under-standing, they can view multiple representations of the content that their peers provide.

Universal Design for Learning (UDL)

Multiple representations, multiple means of expressing understanding, and multiple forms of engagement are at the core of Universal Design for Learning (UDL). UDL strategies were originally designed to help struggling learners, but are also known to benefit all students. Universal Design is an architectural concept that made buildings, products, and environments inherently accessible to people with or without physical disabilities. While design modifications such as ramps and dropped curbs are critical to disabled travelers, they benefit everyone by providing ease of access.

The National Education Technology Plan advocates incorporating UDL "… to develop goals, instructional methods, classroom materials, and assessments [to] improve outcomes for diverse learners by providing fair opportunities for learning by improving access to content" (U.S. Office of Educational Technology, 2011). UDL strategies are at the core of the Special Education training that the San Lorenzo Unified School District offers for collaborative teaching (partnering general education and special education teachers) because these strategies benefit all learners.

Multiple representations support students with different learning modalities, and multiple forms of engagement or participation vary the learning experience. Being able to express understanding creates student buy-in, and technology expands access to tools and a broader audience. A constructivist learning environment actively engages students who work collaboratively to create projects to express their understanding of content. These student-created projects, when added to the research and reference resources, increase multiple representations of the content.

Now What: Empowerment

Learning content is not the end of the unit—it is the gateway to empowering students to discover innovative solutions to unmet needs.

Early in the planning process, teachers should ask themselves: *What do I want my students to do as a result of this unit?* After the unit, teachers should challenge students to use their knowledge to find new ways to do familiar activities. Maybe students will find their new knowledge to be "cool" and want to play with it. Play leads to discovery and innovation. By including play in the process, learning expands to include unmet needs that aren't necessarily part of the problem. Play and innovation help students explore other "now what" questions, such as:

- What can I do now? What do I want to try?

- What can others do now? What can others try now?

- Does this represent an "outside the box" application for something else?

- Can this simplify a question many of us struggle with?

- If I think this is "cool," who else would agree? How can I share this?

This is where the 4Cs and traits that promote innovation come into play. In order to implement new ideas, services, and products, innovators need to be able to collaborate. Collaboration requires communication that stands out from the glut of other media and messages. It must also be creative and withstand critical examination. Critical thinking, when supported by experimentation and observation, spurs new ideas and improvement.

Empathetic Thinking Skills and Design Thinking

Constructivism encourages using higher-order thinking skills of analysis, evaluation, and creativity. If we challenge our students to make a difference with what they have learned, we ask them to employ these skills to innovate.

Making a difference infers that there are users or beneficiaries. In business, users are customers; in education, users are learners. If users are going to be beneficiaries of innovation, innovators must truly understand them and their needs. Innovators must align output with outcome. What is created must address an unmet need, not be just an extension of whimsy, to be a successful innovation. David Kelley calls this user-centric creative process "empathetic design" (2013)

Empathetic thinking is what distinguishes learning in the information age from learning in the Innovation Age. Think about the difference between "create" (higher-order thinking skills) and "creativity" (one of the 4C characteristics of Common Core instruction). In information-age learning, teachers had students create projects to construct meaning. In Innovation Age learning, teachers develop creativity in students to empower them to find solutions to unmet needs.

To be competitive in the Innovation Age, students need to be able to impact their audiences. This assumes that they are designing for an audience, which is the basis for empathetic design. It's not just what they can create, but the impact of their creation. Empathetic design goes beyond tolerance for different perspectives; it capitalizes on multiple perspectives for better, more elegant solutions.

How can teachers ensure that empathetic thinking is infused throughout the learning process?

- **Begin Projects with Empathetic Thinking.** Focus students on the audience for their projects, and make them aware of empathetic design. Their projects will be more powerful and meaningful as a result.

- **Formalize Empathetic Thinking.** As students become more aware of audience and the need for empathetic thinking, make learning about the audience a formal step in the project. Tom Kelley uses an empathy map in the design thinking process at d.school (Hasso Plattner Institute of Design at Stanford). Either alone or in small groups, students use an oversized sheet of paper to map what their target audience says, does, thinks, and feels. The sheet of paper consists of quadrants, starting with "Say" in the top left corner and goes clockwise with "Think" (top right), "Feel" (bottom right), and "Do" (bottom left). They record their observations on adhesive notes and mark trends and contradictions to help identify problems and gaps.

- **Revisions and Iterations.** Focus on the user as adjustments are being made to projects. Revisit user needs with subsequent iterations of the solution.

Play

Getting to the "now what" means educators need to allow time for play. Students need time to be curious, experiment, and explore content and concepts deeply to be able to link the purpose of the content to real-world scenarios. Google is known for allowing employees to explore their own interests during 20% of their day. Many of the most creative apps began during this "play time." Enrichment opportunities that teach students how to create their own games through coding often lead to interest in technology. Middle school students in Dr. Leigh Zeitz's free choice course created Rube Goldberg contraptions for fun (http://www.slide-share.net/zeitz/building-innovative-thikning-through-rube-goldberg-inventions); along the way they deepened their understanding of simple machines, math, and physical science.

In the Innovation Age it's not what you know but what you do with what you know. What are you going to do with what you've just learned? Seeking solutions to unmet needs should be part of all learning. Exploring next steps should become a habit. Challenge your students to experiment with their newly-acquired knowledge and/or technical skill.

Summary

What   To meet the demands of the Innovation Age, teachers should think in terms of what (exposure to basic content and skills), so what (engagement and active learning), and now what (empowerment to make a difference).

So What   Innovation Age teaching goes beyond exposure and engagement; it empowers students to use what they learn in new ways.

Now What   Teachers and students will seek the answers to what, so what, and now what questions to gain clarity, relevance, and innovation skills.

Up Next…

Systemic Classroom Changes

How to implement consistent changes to assessments, technology integration strategies, and extended learning environments to ensure Innovation Age learning.

CHAPTER **3**

Systemic
Classroom Changes

The most dangerous strategy
is to jump a chasm in two leaps.

— Benjamin Disraeli

Thinking in terms of what, so what, and now what puts an Innovation Age spin and clarity around any project or unit of study. But to change the culture of educaton and fully prepare students to thrive in the Innovation Age, it is important to wholeheartedly change the learning environment, employ a technology integration strategy, and make your grading policy iteration-friendly.

Closing the Learning Environment Gap

Innovative learning environments promote collaboration, multidisciplinary learning, thoughtful trial and error, and creativity. In designing learning environments that encourage innovation, frameworks should provide educators with opportunities to join associational, multidisciplinary thinking with creative and thoughtful experimentation in collaborative environments.

Collaboration, multiple perspectives, identification of "outside of the box" unmet needs, and playfulness are critical elements of innovation, but they don't always fit into traditional workspace designs. Most computer labs in our district were designed for test taking and individual skill building; most of our students go to the lab to access technology. The computers are lined against the wall in a U-shape, hardly conducive to collaborative learning. Mobile labs of laptops and Chromebooks have started to replace outdated desktop computers, and proactive teachers have begun lobbying for dedicated carts of mobile devices to integrate technology into their classes daily. Access to technology is only the first step in designing learning environments that are conducive to collaboration, communication, creativity, and critical thinking.

Companies that have become synonymous with innovation, such as Google, Facebook, Pixar, and Yahoo!, have designed their workspaces to reflect their brand and attract innovative people. Design strategies include the use of open floor plans, lighting, color, and music to achieve a playful, creative mood. Companies such as IDEO utilize open community spaces that invite asynchronous contribution of ideas and feedback. Technology is leveraged to expand the physical workspace into virtual workspaces that extend the free flow of information and collaboration. Mobile technologies have blurred workplace boundaries.

In general, physical workspaces that encourage networking among individuals with diverse perspectives produce creative results. Workspaces should be designed to elicit playfulness and a free flow of ideas. Likewise, classrooms should adopt a blended learning environment model to enhance both face-to-face and virtual interaction. Many free technologies are available to expand collaboration and information-sharing capabilities, including resources for authoring interactive media, gaming, and digital instruction.

In *Creating Innovators* (2012), Tony Wagner noticed common characteristics in learning environments which focus on innovation that are similar to those identified in *The Innovator's DNA* (2011). These environments promoted collaboration, multidisciplinary learning, thoughtful trial and error, and creativity. Environments that encourage innovation should include an understanding for skills that enhance the innovation process. They must provide opportunities for associational, multidisciplinary thinking with creative and thoughtful experimentation.

If you frequently use constructivist learning strategies in your classroom, you are more likely to see innovation-friendly elements in play. If your learning environment uses technologies more frequently for instructional purposes than for student-centered projects, you provide a less constructivist environment. Districts with a high degree of collaboration, flexibility, transparency, and avenues for community input are more likely to be open to innovation and positive change.

Teachers who have to rely on computer lab time or have to check out a cart of devices to integrate technology into their lessons suffer from a "learning environment gap." When teachers face a day-to-day or topic-to-topic learning environment gap, their classrooms are not consistently configured for 4Cs or tech-infused learning. Without consistent or reliable access, it is difficult to expect teachers to embrace technology.

To prevent a home-to-school learning environment gap, teachers can design extended or blended (combination of face-to-face and online) learning so students and their support network can have continuous access to curriculum resources. Many free and paid virtual classroom tools exist, including learning management systems (LMS), curriculum management systems (CMS), or virtual classrooms, such as Google Classroom, Edmodo, Collaborize Classroom, and Edu 2.0.

At the secondary level, students experience a subject-to-subject learning environment gap when only some of their teachers provide access to technology or understand how to integrate it into their classroom. Consistency is necessary to build a learning culture; gaps prevent this from developing.

Systematic Technology Integration

Listing dual learning outcomes calls attention to technology learning outcomes as well as to content knowledge and skills. Teachers can leverage technology even more strategically if they map out technology integration in terms of a continuum of skills and a variety of instructional uses.

Continuum of Skills

Teaching technology skills as a continuum of scaffolded skills, as opposed to "just in time learning," prevents frustration in many students, adults and kids alike. Figure 3.1 shows the continuum of multimedia skills that was used in an "Enhancing Visual Learning through Media and Technology" workshop I facilitated during the 2014 Summer Technology Academies at San Lorenzo Unified School District. The subject of visual learning was explored first through the gathering of images. Editing and drawing tools were introduced and images from the previous lessons were edited and inserted into drawings. The next installment of visual learning content involved presentation, featuring a slide show project as well as a quick lesson on creating and editing sound files using Audacity (free sound-editing software). This set the stage for animation and video editing. In a yearlong class, teachers can spread out these projects over months so students can more easily create increasingly complex projects and focus on content.

This scaffolded planning approach is beneficial because it builds a solid base of technology skills that are refined and built upon. It can also be applied to other skill areas, such as developing writing skills, data and spreadsheet proficiency, and publication.

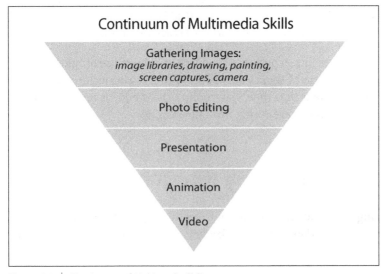

Figure 3.1 | Continuum of Multimedia Skills.

Instructional Uses

When the Common Core State Standards were introduced in California, districts were given funding to ensure readiness for online testing. Constructivist and project-based learning advocates secured technology tools for student production. The subsequent systematic integration of technology has helped to expand the use of technology tools in educational settings. An example of this can be seen in the Google Play for Education teacher access portal. Teachers can select tools or subject areas from the left navigation and refine their search based on intended uses. The current list includes Teacher Tool, Instruction, Reference/Research, Review/Drill, Student Tool, and Differentiation.

Another systematic approach is to map technology uses against thinking skills and the three levels of thinking that encourage student empowerment (shown in Table 3.1). How could you systematically incorporate the tools in the right column? Does the list present new opportunities for your students?

Table 3.1 | Thinking skills and technology tools

Now What?	
	Student voice: publication tools, blogs, social media
Empowerment	Student journals: word processing, ePortfolio tools, blogs
	Crowd sourcing
Metacognition: learning how to learn	Concept mapping tools, virtual whiteboards
Innovation: finding solutions to unmet needs	Simulation tools
Lower-Order Thinking Skills	Skill-builders, flash card tools
• Remember	Production tools
• Understand	Problem-solving games, content support websites such as Khan Academy
• Apply	Coding tools
Higher-Order Thinking Skills	Multimedia and 3D tools
• Analysis	Research and reference tools
• Evaluation	Notetaking and reporting, forms and survey tools
• Creativity or Creation	Chat, videoconferencing, such as FaceTime, Skype, Google Hangouts
Empathetic Thinking Skills	Prototyping, CAD software
• Understanding user	Organizational aids, calendaring
• Understanding problems	Differentiation and assistive technologies
• Designing a solution from multiple perspectives	

Iteration-Friendly Assessment

Grades matter. Student assessment matters. If innovation matters, is your grade book iteration-friendly? Does it reward grit, perseverance, risk, and learning from mistakes?

Evidence that grades matter is everywhere. Report cards are displayed on refrigerators, proud parents sport "My kid is an honor student" bumper stickers, and share how their children earned awards for distinguishing themselves. Grades are becoming more valued than SAT and ACT scores for some college applications (Westervelt, 2014). An emphasis on good grades can be detrimental and prevent students from excelling in other areas or measuring success in different ways.

Innovation requires an iterative process. Very few startups, new products and services, and organizational change would happen if immediate, consistent success was required. Grades have to be iteration-friendly if educators are to nurture students who will thrive in the Innovation Age.

Aligning Assessment with Dual Learning Outcomes

Each learning outcome needs to have a metric for success. How do we know that the outcome was realized? Some outcomes can be checked off as done or not done. Other outcomes are evaluated through a system of points, which yields a range of proficiency.

In the dissertation study, the dual learning outcomes were evaluated in different ways. For high school students who are dependent on grades for college entrance and career opportunities, it is especially important to balance the weight given to each outcome.

Students and parents measure success through grades and scores on assessments. A variety and balance of assessments can reflect mastery learning, persistence, experimentation, and other Innovation Age skills. Teachers, particularly single-subject teachers like the Biology teacher in the dissertation study, are often uncomfortable about evaluating or grading technology projects. There are several conflicting ideologies:

- Grades vs. assessments

- Process vs. product

- Teacher-evaluation vs. self-evaluation

- Teacher-created rubric vs. group-created rubric

- Intrinsic motivation vs. extrinsic motivation

- Formative vs. summative assessments

- Content-based assessments vs. performance tasks

- "What matters is assessed" vs. "What is assessed matters"

The truth of the matter is that we use multiple measures to get a picture of student achievement. What does success look like? It looks different from different angles. With teacher-centered, didactic instruction, assessments focus on measuring how much information students retain. In the Innovation Age, critical thinking, creativity, and collaboration have become part of learning, and that kind of learning is harder to measure. Assessment of learning is not limited to grades, standardized tests, and performance tasks alone; it will come from the students' peers and the global community.

Assessment Of, For, and As Learning

Teachers often struggle to balance instructional minutes and assessment minutes. If we replace "versus" with "and/with," we get a blend of assessments, and we can "develop assessment of, for, and as learning" (Ainsworth, 2011). Assessments do not always fall neatly into the three categories, nor is there a need to make clear distinctions.

It helped me to create the following list of assessment qualities, below, to better understand how assessment can extend beyond judgment of skill mastery and effort to become a learning and teaching tool.

Assessment of learning

- Summative

- Teacher-assigned

- Criterion-normed, product-based

- Used in grades

- Extrinsic motivation

Balancing Multiple Measures

In the Advanced Biology unit for the dissertation study, there were four graded activities: a 20-pt concept map, a 50-pt eModule, a 20-pt learning journal, and a 74-pt unit test. What could this point assignment mean to students?

At face value the unit test comprises 45% of the total possible points, which reflects a priority on learning the IB Advanced Biology content. The eModule was worth up to 50 points (31% of the total), as evaluated against the standards established on the syllabus. The teacher graded the eModule summatively, but students assessed their daily progress on it and helped each other debug their modules. The 20-pt concept map and 20-pt individual learning journal were equal in points (12% each) and involved both formative self-assessment and summative teacher-assessment. Figure 3.2 displays the weight of each activity based on raw point value, which may reflect the teacher's priorities from the student's perspective.

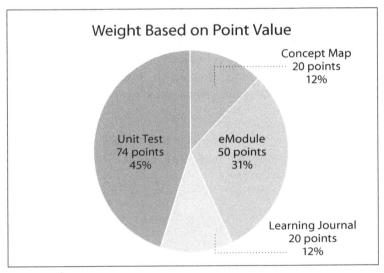

Figure 3.2 | Weight based on point value.

Although the "assessment of, for, and as learning" concept did not factor into the construction of the instructional strategy, it is interesting to examine the unit assessments retrospectively through that lens. The 74-pt multiple choice and short essay unit exam was clearly an example of "assessment of" the learning of biology concepts.

The dissertation study syllabus listed the following descriptions of Interactive Media (eModule) and grading rubric:

Description of Interactive Media

- Set up the problem

- Research DNA replication and protein synthesis using texts, animations, etc., in groups

- Plan the eLearning module (Inspiration)

- Integrate technology into the presentation using Adobe Captivate 2 and Flash 8

- Suggest resources for biology, technology tutorials

Grading Rubric for Interactive Media Project

- Establish the problem

- Quality of research on stages of mitosis and cell cycle, including cancer

- Storyboard/concept map of eLearning module

- Interactive media presentation

Judging by the description, the 50-pt eModule was graded summatively on both the biology content and the technical components. There is a blend of "assessment of" the learning of biology and technology that was graded, and the ungraded self-assessment "as" developmental learning during the debugging phase of the eModule project.

The 20-pt concept map was also graded by the teacher for biology content and the ability to produce a concept map using technology. It was described as part of the eModule project, and represents a similar blend of assessment of and for learning.

When you combine the 20 points for the concept map and 50 points for the eModule, they total 70 points, or 33%.

The learning journal was designed to promote ongoing student reflection and self-assessment. It can be considered "assessment for" and "as" learning. Although a grading criterion was included on the syllabus, students received points for turning in journals regardless of the quality of the entries because 1) the intended purpose of individual accountability and reflection were accomplished when students made their posts, 2) there were time constraints for grading, and 3) the grading rubric was not well established.

Students in the study were not graded for the quality of the questions that they included in the eModules, but when students develop questions for assessment it is a form of formative assessment because it reflects their analysis of important concepts and common misconceptions. Based on his research, Wiliam states, "This can be a particularly effective strategy with disaffected older students, who often feel threatened by tests. Writing a test for the topic they have completed, and knowing that the teacher is going to grade the questions rather than the answer, can be hugely liberating for many students" (Wiliam, 2011, p.68).

It is difficult to determine the balance between formative and summative assessment. In the grade book, this unit consisted of largely summative, teacher-assigned assessment. The student-created, self-correcting quizzes included in their eModules are a good example of informal formative assessments that teachers use to gauge student learning. Many digital age learning skills are considered "soft skills," which can easily go unassessed. Teachers should consider assessment tools that include criteria for identifying soft skills.

Performance Task Assessment

Many constructivist classrooms incorporate performance tasks to promote soft skills, such as critical thinking, collaboration, and innovation. The North Central Regional Educational Laboratory (NCREL) defines a "performance task" as "an assessment exercise that is goal directed. The exercise is developed to elicit students' application of a wide range of skills and knowledge to solve a complex problem" (http://NCREL.org). If tasks are activities that students complete to demonstrate understanding, then constructivist projects qualify under the broad definition of performance tasks. Constructivist performance tasks produce a range of solutions that demonstrate deep understanding rather than a single right answer. The simpler the task, the simpler the solution; more complex tasks require complex solutions (ETS, 2006).

Performance tasks help students make sense of what they are learning, think independently, work collaboratively, make connections to other areas of study, and persevere—skills they are sure to need in life after high school. Performance tasks are the remedy for student boredom and disengagement. Further, such tasks promote "deeper learning" and require more time to implement. Understanding by Design (UbD) performance tasks identify criteria for evidence of varying levels of understanding (Ainsworth, 2011).

"Performance task assessment" has come to have multiple meanings. Using a broad definition of performance task, a performance task assessment is a set of criteria, often in the form of a rubric. Student-centered technology-infused instructional strategies, such as student-authored interactive media described in Chapters One through Three, could be peer- or self-evaluated using performance task criteria rubrics. It is important to find the balance between being clear about expectations and being too explicit, which limits the creativity and depth of thinking. "The clearer you are about what you want, the more likely you are to get it, but the less likely it is to mean anything" (Wiliam, 2011, p. 60). Building in a degree of generality into rubrics promotes transfer, which indicates that students can apply their learning to other contexts. Wiliam also suggests that students help structure the rubrics to encourage buy-in and deeper understanding of the learning goals and outcomes.

"Performance task assessment" is taking on a more specific definition of assessment questions, which require students to provide essay-type answers to open-ended questions. Both Common Core assessment consortia, PARC and SMARTER-Balanced, have designed assessments that include performance task items scored by computer based on a rubric.

My point is that no matter what kind of assessment strategies you employ, take a moment to step back and evaluate the priorities you are communicating to your students. Confirm that the point values you assign accurately reflect the balance between standards-based learning and soft skill, digital age learning; formative and summative assessment; teacher-evaluated grades and self-assessment; assessment of, for, and as learning. If you are not already familiar with performance task assessment, take a moment to see how it lends itself to constructivist learning in the Innovation Age.

Summary

What   Learning environments, technology integration, and assessment policies need to be consistent to be effective.

So What   Changes made in classrooms to bridge the chasm between information-age and Innovation Age learning need to be made systemically.

Now What   Teachers make consistent changes in their classroom environments, tech integration strategies, and assessment systems to encourage innovation skills.

Up Next...

Empowering Students through the 4Cs

Make the abstract concrete through technology-infused activities that build collaboration, communication, creativity, critical thinking, and innovation skills.

PART II

Empowering Students through the 4Cs

Tell me and I forget. Teach me and I remember.
Involve me and I learn."

— Benjamin Franklin

Part Two takes exposure to the theory of Innovation Age teaching and turns it into concrete action. Teachers across the country are currently implementing the 4Cs of Common Core (collaboration, communication, creativity, and critical thinking). We must engage them to infuse Innovation Age instructional strategies into the 4Cs.

Chapter 4 Collaboration

Innovation Age collaboration is a far cry from old-school group work. Observe collaborative learning. Encourage networking while ensuring accountability.

Chapter 5 Communication

Explore one-way, two-way, and three-dimensional communication. One-way presentational and expressive arts are important, but in this age of interactive media we need to give students the opportunity to use interactive media to involve their audiences. Effective Innovation Age communication is at least three-dimensional, involving communicating through words, data, and graphics.

Chapter 6 Creativity

Encourage creativity to support collaboration and foster the Innovation Age skill of associational thinking. Go beyond higher-order thinking skills and help your students become empathetic thinkers.

Chapter 7 Critical Thinking

Deepen critical thinking by strengthening students' questioning, experimentation, and iterative learning skills.

CHAPTER 4

Collaboration

Most great learning happens in groups.
Collaboration is the stuff of growth.

— Sir Ken Robinson

Collaboration has become a hallmark of the Innovation Age. It is one of the 4Cs, a 21st-century skill, and central to design thinking. If collaboration involved simply getting people together to work on problems at the same time, it would not be considered a real skill. As Sir Ken Robinson puts it, collaboration is the stuff of growth. Networking is often thought of as the act of connecting with other people in the same or related fields. Once it was accepted as part of the innovator's DNA, networking was seen as a way to connect differing perspectives and disciplines. This cross-pollination leads to discovery, not just delivery of product.

Businessman Don Tapscott is quoted as saying, "Collaboration is important not just because it's a better way to learn. The spirit of collaboration is penetrating every institution and all of our lives. So learning to collaborate is part of equipping yourself for effectiveness, problem solving, innovation and life-long learning in an ever-changing networked economy" (Tapscott, 2013). Vygotsky (1978) believed that "What children can do with the assistance of others might be in some sense more indicative of their mental development than what they can do alone."

Collaboration increases the scope of what individuals are capable of learning alone (Edwards, Carr, & Siegel, 2006; Lyle, 2000; Quinn, 2005). Collaboration is not group work where the goal is to divide and conquer. A common pitfall with group work is that one student does the lion's share of the work because he or she cares about the grade. In groups of conscientious members, the project appears disjointed because they lack the time or discipline to use a common voice or format. Each member frequently only knows their portion of the project because the process does not reward or support free flow of ideas or cohesiveness. Parents get irate when their child did all the work and other students get equal credit.

True collaboration occurs when the whole is greater than the sum of the parts; a group can achieve what a single person cannot. So how can teachers foster collaboration in their classrooms, beyond their classrooms, and beyond school? This chapter offers ideas and concrete examples of how you can create a culture of collegial learning and a blended learning environment to enhance your students' collaboration skills.

Creating a Culture of Learning Together

Learning together takes more than being assigned to the same classroom or group. In the words of baseball legend Casey Stengel, "Gettin' good players is easy. Gettin' 'em to play together is the hard part."

Teachers do not have to provide all of the expertise in the classroom, but it is a good idea to try to produce the project yourself in advance to make sure the necessary resources are available to your students. The participating teacher commented that it would also be a plus if the teacher could be "tech-savvy." I interpret being tech-savvy as having the confidence to figure things out. If teachers were to use installed, industry-standard software to replicate the study, I agree that it would be important to ensure that the software was properly installed and operational. Today there are many cloud-based Web 2.0 tools that can create interactive media components or modules, precluding the need to install software prior to the unit.

"Constructivist teaching and learning acknowledges that the teacher and the students are both contributing players in a teaching-learning relationship, and that both bring prior knowledge and experiences into the learning environment" (Morphew, 2012, p. 48). We truly limit our students and ourselves when we only use tools that we feel expert in using. I believe teachers have a responsibility to be prepared but open to learning as part of the community as well. Good teachers are lifelong learners; they should be eager to learn from students.

The student-student dynamic is central to learning together. Students need guidance to collaborate effectively. A collaborative project involves students working together, using their multiple perspectives to find an engaging, user-oriented solution. In today's media-rich world, an audience demands interactivity of some kind. Creating interactive presentations within the constraints of the curricular calendar necessitates a teacher/student dynamic that provides students experience applying collective intelligence. Challenging students to seek an innovative solution to a problem adds a layer of learning if innovation skills are touted.

As I mentioned in Chapter 2, students in the dissertation study commented about the benefits of working together to evaluate their experience creating interactive eModules. There was evidence of learning together within groups as well as between groups. Positive responses were found in every subgroup.

A student who started with a high initial score stated,

> My group worked really well together. We continually bounced ideas off each [other] to reorganize our presentation to make the most sense.

A "big gainer" also endorsed the group work aspect of the instructional strategy, stating,

> My experience was good because my group and I were able to work well together. Even though we often did not know how to use the program we were often able to use our books to guide us. The brainstorm also kept our ideas organized so we could keep on track.

A student with a low initial score reported,

> In our group we fed off each other. While everyone took turns working on the computers, I was the one who knew how to work the computer, so I mostly contributed that way. Another person in our group knew the curriculum pretty well, but if she didn't know something for sure the other girl could help. Being with them I was able to learn quite a lot.

A student who was not part of any subgroup identified the advantages of group work by writing,

> Working in groups made it easier, because it allowed you to discuss the topic and if you didn't understand something, you could just ask someone in the group.

Students can create more engaging curriculum units for their peers than adults (Zhao, 2012). Building a curriculum that really interests students is difficult because educators are of a different generation. If we build it, they may not necessarily like it or learn. If THEY build it, students will understand the content more deeply, use technology tools more adroitly, and gain authentic innovation curriculum experience. Students who author peer-teaching curriculum give their projects purpose and intrinsic motivation to design higher-quality products. Yong Zhao and the University of Oregon developed Oba (www.obaworld.net), a full suite of tools designed to help students produce digital curriculum and reach a global market. It was developed to provide tools for online course management, networking, portfolio management, video editing and storage, and free virtual meeting spaces for students and educators. Applying online technology tools for learning and promoting entrepreneurship takes peer teaching to a whole new level!

A team's makeup impacts its ability to succeed. The tendency in schools is to put comparable students together so they can move at the same pace. This makes sense for direct instruction, because likeness narrows the range of ability and the need for differentiation. But in project-based learning and honing Innovation Age skills, it takes a broad spectrum of stakeholders with multiple perspectives. Innovators invite feedback from many different people in many different roles so they can anticipate a broader range of strengths and weaknesses in their products. In super creative, cutting-edge workplaces such as IDEO and Amazon, projects are posted in highly-trafficked places to solicit a broad range of feedback.

It would be chaos if work groups always had to be diverse. In creating a culture of collaboration, it is important to have fluid groupings. If we revisit Modi's Innovation Life Cycle, you can see where like and disparate groupings make sense.

1. **Ideation.** Ideas are submitted, discussed, and rated.
   Ideas are submitted by individuals or small groups, but multiple perspectives are useful to discuss and rate ideas.

2. **Selection.** The "best" ideas are selected and moved into the process.
   The selection requires multiple perspectives.

3. **Inception.** Selected ideas are developed.
   When ideas are developed to a high degree of detail, the work is usually done by a team of experts with similar perspectives and expertise.

4. **Presentation.** Selected ideas are presented to stakeholders.
   The presentation is done by the expert group if the team can communicate persuasively through words, data, and graphics. (More on this multidimensional communication in Chapter 5.) The stakeholder group should be diverse and represent multiple perspectives.

5. **Elaboration.** Projects that are selected by stakeholders are aligned with projected milestones/goals and timeline.
   Elaboration goes back to the expert group with the addition of a project manager and additional staff, per the needs of the development team and available funding.

6. **Transition.** Implementation of product, prototype, or demonstration of innovation.

The takeaway for teachers is to encourage a culture of collaborative learning where small groups feel free to network with other groups for feedback and support. A range of perspectives and skills should be welcomed. Students in the dissertation study worked in groups of two or three, but based on their journal notes and exit surveys it is clear that they benefitted from working as a classroom community.

Ensuring accountability while encouraging collaboration means finding a balance in your grading. Achieving a balance among individual contribution, collaborative projects/products, personal reflection, incremental due dates, and content mastery may be one, albeit challenging, solution. It is important to reward process as well as product to develop a collaborative culture.

We've covered the need to develop collaboration skills, encourage networking, and design learning environments that are conducive to innovation. Now let's look at how teachers can foster collaboration in class, beyond class, and beyond school.

Collaboration in Class

In 2014, when I facilitated the Summer Technology Academies workshop,"Using Google Apps for Education to Implement the Common Core," at the San Lorenzo Unified School District in California, many teachers still were not sold on the benefits of student collaboration. (For more details about the Summer Tech Academies, see Chapter 9.) I'm sure they had their reasons: bad experiences with group work, "been there, done that," too much wasted time, unfair assessment, and so on.

If I were to ask teachers to develop collaboration skills in their students, I needed to "walk that talk." Research is one of the infused skills in Common Core instruction so I chose to immerse them in a collaborative task: create a list of 10 research tips for their students. Before you skip to the next section, please note that the overwhelming majority of teachers were pleasantly surprised when they learned more from the process and their colleagues than they expected. They also agreed that no matter how good my presentation might have been, I could not have provided the same variety of approaches to targeted research tips and instructional strategies on my own. Nothing personal—collaboration is just that powerful!

Table 4.1 shows a summary of the steps and takeaways from the three sessions of "Using Google Apps for Education to Implement the Common Core."

The Google Apps for Education (GAFE) domain is new for our district. It has been a game-changing tool for students, teachers, and leadership at all levels, who have started to leverage the simultaneous editing and document-sharing capabilities that Google Apps offer. I have started Google Apps workshops for the Educational Leadership Team, all principals and assistant principals, teachers on special assignment, our three union presidents, and clerical support staff. Within the first years of deployment, I will have worked with the Board of Trustees, directors and managers of business services, and most counselors, psychologists, and coordinators. We focused on sharing folders, Docs, and Presentations. As we move through the other Cs I plan to integrate the use of Forms, Spreadsheets, and Drawing.

Table 4.1 | Takeaways and assignments from Summer Technology Academy

Concept: Enhance your collaborative learning strategies while creating a list of research tips to share with your students.

Takeaway	Assignment
Empathetic thinking: Frame your research so students find it useful. What results do you want from them?	1. Start with your target audience in mind (empathetic thinking).
Everyone can contribute something to the mix no matter how little prior knowledge they have.	2. Independent research: build in time so every team member can bring an idea to the group. (10 minutes)
Honor every contribution and develop a "50 solutions" mentality. Incremental Accountability: Ask each group to submit draft of 50 solutions.	3. Encourage creativity and openness by posing a seemingly impossible goal: after individual preliminary searches ask each group to compile 50 research tips. Build tech skills in Google Presentation app, sharing slides, copying/pasting simultaneously, incremental accountability. (20 minutes)
Instead of doing a gallery walk of ideas and voting with stickers, use virtual stickers on a presentation.	4. Whittle the list down to the top 10 via discussion, voting ("stickers" using Google Drawing Tools), and editing current slides. A lot of analysis takes place in order to maximize the 3 minutes allowed. (15 minutes)
If Letterman can list his top 10 in less than three minutes, you can too. Concision is an art. Mark Twain once said, "… if I had more time I would've written you a shorter letter."	5. 3-minute group presentations (use a timer). Each group shares presentation with workshop leader. Files sorted by "last modified" so most recent files move to the top. The URL is assigned to the file so it doesn't change if/when the file is moved. (3 minutes x number of groups)
Use the minute between presentations for positive affirmations for previous groups.	6. The teacher/judges debrief as groups get ready. What did you like about the presentation? What was unique about their work?

Using cloud-based applications such as Google Docs, Dropbox, Evernote, wikis, and blogs can eliminate the need for multiple copies. Users can share access to documents to allow real-time collaborative writing. In spring 2015, we also deployed Microsoft Office 365 to provide staff and students access to OneNote Class, One Drive, and familiar Office applications online.

Collaboration beyond Class

Learning together extends beyond physical space and time in the Innovation Age. If the resources available to students are housed in a learning management system (LMS) or intranet portal, students can continue to work collaboratively outside of class.

We had planned to use a district-provided intranet portal that would allow students to post questions and share expertise via a threaded discussion board, share documents and links, and make journal entries in a protected environment. They would have had the benefits of daily face-to-face class sessions and collaboration tools of a distance learning environment. The portal was not completely functional when the study ran, so students turned their journals in to a digital drop box.

Free Course Management Systems (CMS)

Following are some examples of course management systems that are free to use.

- **Google Classroom.** Create a virtual classroom that allows you to enroll or invite students and attach documents from your Google Drive for them to view or edit and submit copies back to you. If you have an account in an education domain, you will find the Classroom App by clicking your app icon > Scroll down to "even more from Google." *http://classroom.google.com*

- **Moodle.** Create online learning site: *http://moodle.org*

- **Schoolrack.** Free classroom blog, discussion board, portal, etc.: *http://schoolrack.com*

- **Schoology.** Integration, collaboration, and data tools: *http://schoology.com*

- **Oba.** Cloud collaboration, development and learning: *http://obaworld.net*

- **Edu 2.0.** Virtual school, collaboration tools: *http://edu20.org*

- **CourseSites.** Free offering of Blackboard: *http://coursesites.com*

- **Edmodo.** Connecting learners with people and resources: *http://edmodo.com*

If we were to replicate the study today, we could choose from more than 100 LMSs, including free LMS options. Some school web-hosting services include LMS options in their package of services.

Combining face-to-face learning with online components is popularly called blended learning. According to the Innosight Institute (Horn & Staker, 2011), "Blended learning has the potential to revolutionize K–12 education in terms of quality and cost because it allows for a more consistent and personalized pedagogy, requires fewer specialized teachers, and uses space efficiently." In their 2012 report, Innosight Institute classified blended learning environments into four basic models:

- **Rotation model** (includes station-rotation model, lab-rotation model, flipped-classroom model, and individual-rotation model). Students rotate on a fixed schedule or at the teacher's discretion.

- **Flex model.** Students progress on an individually customized, fluid schedule.

- **Self-Blend model.** Students choose to take one or more courses entirely online.

- **Enriched-Virtual model.** Mostly virtual school experience with some classroom experiences.

Choosing a blended learning model should begin with an educational goal. Next, determine the target groups and the district's capabilities and needs (Watson, Murin, Vashaw, Gemin, & Rapp, 2011). The Evergreen Education Group provides a comprehensive guide based on an annually updated review of policy and practice and posts a free downloadable file online at http://kpk12.com. I recommend it as a resource for studying the feasibility of a district-wide LMS or blended learning model.

The instructional strategy of student-authored interactive media described in Chapter 3 would fall largely in the face-to-face setting, with few online resources and communication. It is closest to the traditional face-to-face model on the blended learning continuum, where completely face-to-face is at one end and completely online is at the other (Watson, 2008). The strategy can be modified to fit any model of blended learning.

In case you were thinking blended learning is for the adventurous few, you may be surprised to learn that providing virtual environments was included in the ISTE Standards for Teachers. To help "facilitate and inspire student learning and creativity," Standard One states that teachers should provide "both face-to-face and virtual environments" (ISTE, 2008). ISTE essentially advocates a blended learning environment, which may range from a mainly traditional face-to-face setting with few online resources or communication to mainly online with options for face-to-face instruction.

Collaboration beyond School

The LMS—Learning Management System or customized online classroom—is only part of the blended learning environment. There are hundreds of learning resources outside the school and classroom that educators can incorporate to enhance their collaborative learning environments. Students can research any topic, data, tutorials regarding software applications and apps, Ask an Expert, and more. Teachers can expedite the search process by giving students links to reliable content-related resources. Mobile apps can provide practice for lower-level thinking skills and drills. Online standards-based content runs the gamut from free supplemental resources to fully online courses.

Educational Technology Resources

Educators can also draw on the many digital options to educational technology, as well as material in print. Per their comfort level and personal preferences, educators can sign up for newsletters, news feeds using Really Simple Syndication (RSS), webinars, threaded discussions, online tech courses, and networking sites like Ning. There are teams of people working full time on websites and blogs that try to stay current with the myriad resources and trends, and it is still not enough. Do check out these sites:

Edudemic. www.edudemic.com
View posts on technology tools by filtering them by category and sorting them by date, title, and number of views. Some example articles are "The 100 Best Video Sites for Educators," "The 100 Best Web 2.0 Classroom Tools

Chosen by You," "7 Online Quiz Tools Perfect for Classrooms," or "Five Free Apps for Classrooms with a Single iPad."

Educational Technology and Mobile Learning. www.educatorstechnology.com
A resource of educational web tools and mobile apps for teachers and educators.

eSchool News. www.eschoolnews.com
Technology news for today's K-20 educator. The website produces new articles almost daily, with an archive of past issues. Features of the site include an educator resource center, resources, webinars, and funding opportunities.

International Society for Technology in Education (ISTE). www.iste.org
An invaluable array of resources, including timely research and professional learning (networking, books, webinars, annual conferences). Also includes standards for students, teachers, administrators, coaches, and computer science educators.

Social Media

Social media has become ubiquitous as organizations harness the power of its reach to build sales, awareness, and relationships. It is common to find links to share or "like" websites via the personal networking sites, such as Facebook, Google +1, Twitter, Linked In, and Pinterest. Collective intelligence sites in the form of wikis and blogs help individuals communicate with potentially vast audiences. Teenagers continue to use social media often (Pew Internet, 2011), with 82% of 14- to 17-year-olds and 55% of 12- to 13-year-olds in the 2009 survey reporting they visited sites daily.

While social media has increased expression and creativity outside of school, Bull et al. (2008) site numerous constraints that prevent schools from capitalizing on the tools: 1) school content must address specific learning objectives, 2) time constraints, 3) adding technology can increase the complexity of classroom management, 4) access to online media tools is often constrained, 5) teachers have few models for effective media integration, and 6) limited research is available on best practices.

In a report on how social media is used in higher education, Moran, Seaman, and Tinti-Kane (2011) state that while they believe "social media sites are valuable tools for collaborative learning," faculty are most concerned about the time social media will require, a lack of integrity of student submissions, and privacy. Social media tools for student authoring include wikis, blogs, Facebook, Twitter, Pinterest, and Google+.

Wikis

Wikis are web pages that are cooperatively and collaboratively written so that multiple perspectives can be presented in a single website. Perhaps the most famous wiki is Wikipedia. Wikis are generally public, but can be limited to classes when they are part of a password-protected LMS. Students may use wikis for: 1) group-authored research projects, 2) summaries after readings as a form of discussion, 3) creating an annotated group bibliography, 4) brainstorming and concept-mapping, and 5) as a presentational tool (Parker & Chao, 2007).

Blogs

Benefits of blogs include: 1) learning can continue outside the classroom, 2) students with diverse opinions and interests are connected, 3) they encourage critical thinking and respect for other perspectives, 4) they promote sharing of knowledge, creativity, communication, and self-expression, 5) they create an opportunity to use new technologies, and 6) they allow students and instructors from different courses to learn together (Lujan-Mora & Juana-Espinosa, 2007). Blogs are also commonly included in CMS and LMS tools.

Facebook

Facebook is the largest social network site; it can be an effective education tool if used thoughtfully. Teachers can create groups for their classes and set them as closed. Once a group is set, Facebook can be used to share media, communicate with the class regarding projects and assignments, send messages, and collaborate. Teachers can add apps for students, including: WeRead for book discussions, Notely for organizing assignments and notes, Study Groups for collaboration, and CiteMe for learning how to cite resources properly (www.educatorstechnology. com). Students can establish Fan Pages for organizations that are separate from their personal profiles.

Twitter

Twitter has exploded as a discussion tool. Edudemic posted a pretty comprehensive list of over 300 education-related discussion topics of 2012. Any user can add a hashtag (#) to mark keywords or topics in a tweet. By using a hashtag the tweet can appear in search results or discussion monitoring. A great tip to prevent wearing out all of your followers is to hide hashtag tweets by starting with @hidetag.

Pinterest

Pinterest is a digital bulletin board that allows users to share and collect photos of their favorite interests and events. It is the third-fastest growing social network, behind Facebook and Twitter.

Google+

Google+ is also available as an option in the Education Suite. Like Gmail and Calendar, this feature can be turned on for specific organizational units in the Google domain. Students can use Google+ as a space to hangout, create groups, and share.

Web and Videoconferencing

Videoconferencing is now more accessible than ever with web tools such as Skype, WebEx, GoToMeeting, and Google Hangouts. It is no longer reserved for teachers who have access to dedicated videoconferencing equipment. Videoconferencing extends collaboration beyond school in the form of Ask an Expert, virtual field trips, distance learning, distance partnerships, and more.

We have come full circle in this discussion about collaboration. We agree that collaboration is a skill that our Innovation Age students need to develop, but it is up to their teachers to make it work. Effective collaboration takes forethought and planning—from designing the learning environment to defining the outcomes and tasks, and gathering the necessary resources. Why should this activity be done collaboratively? Are the appropriate stakeholders invited to participate? How do we make effective use of time and ideas?

Summary

What   In the Innovation Age, students need learning environments that foster collaboration and networking.

So What   Collaborative learning environments provide a culture of learning together, multiple perspectives, and opportunities to continue beyond the confines of the classroom.

Now What   Teachers will develop collaborative learning environments that encourage learning in class, beyond class, and beyond school.

Up Next...

Communication

Effective collaboration requires communication through words, graphics, and data.

CHAPTER **5**

Communication

> You can have brilliant ideas, but if you can't get them across,
> your ideas won't get you anywhere.
>
> — Lee Iacocca

Communication is the art of conveying ideas, and like all skills, communication comes from observation, clear intent, and a sense of openness. We cannot collaborate without communication. It is such a complex field that one could make a profession of it, and make the mastery of it a lifetime pursuit. As a former advertising executive and frustrated graphic artist, I would like to delve into the art of communication. Instead I want to address communication in terms of teaching and learning in the Innovation Age.

Observation is one of the five skills Dyer, Gregersen, and Christensen identified as part of *The Innovator's DNA* (2011). While keen observation is an inseparable part of creativity and critical thinking, I chose to include it in the context of communication. Whether we choose to use one-way presentational communication, two-way interactive communication, or enhanced 3D communication depends on our audience and what we want to communicate.

My observation has been that information-age communication has largely been one-way and presentational. In the 1990s technology and personal computers made it possible for the global public to connect quickly and easily. Pioneering teachers could empower students with the ability to use word processing, and create slide presentations and videos. Along with information overload came media overload; memorable communication added the dimension of interactivity to engage its audiences. The standard in the Innovation Age is interactive, two-way communication, but most student projects are still presentational in nature. They are not expected to engage their audiences and elicit their responses. As we taught students to communicate, we focused on four communication tools—words, data, multimedia, and graphics—but generally not all in concert. If students are to thrive in the Innovation Age they need to get their ideas across to as broad an audience or market as they can. They will need to leverage multidimensional communication to be able to reach people through multiple modalities, not just fellow right-brain or left-brain thinkers.

This chapter focuses on communication in the Innovation Age from a teacher's perspective, using discussion and project examples to develop and encourage student aptitude for:

- Audience, observation, and openness

- One-way, presentational communication

- Two-way, interactive communication, and

- Three-dimensional communication—words, data, and graphics

Audience, Observation, and Openness

There is a fine line between being observant and easily distracted. When I was teaching, getting my students to focus was a full-time proposition. Whether fourth graders or algebra students, they were easily distracted. I confess that I am often easily distracted. Per the Pixar film *Up!*, "squirrel!" Although we may be tempted to resort to creating blinders for our students, we need to improve their powers of observation so they can excel in the Innovation Age. Let's agree that communication is a means of connecting people and places or an exchange of ideas and information. Communication without an understanding of audience, observation, and media is ineffective.

Audience

Who we are communicating with should determine our approach, but many student assignments are unclear who their audience is other than the teacher. Teachers are not able to respond to every form of student communication (written, verbal, or non-verbal) so students need to be able to identify and target different audiences. Otherwise, they are constantly in "spray and pray" mode, which will not produce effective communication.

Identifying and understanding one's audience is the first step in communication. In advertising it starts with understanding the demographics: who is the target audience; what is their need; what is our solution; how do we capture their attention to move them to action? In a classroom this translates to: who is my audience; what is our common goal; what am I trying to communicate; and how will I know that the idea, information, or news was conveyed?

The prompts what, so what, and now what initiate communication from the audience's perspective. They require empathetic thinking. Table 5.1 compares these communication triggers from two perspectives, marketing versus student communication.

Table 5.1 | Marketing vs. Student Communication

	Marketing	Student Communication
Audience	Who is the target audience?	Who is my audience?
What	What is their need?	What is our common goal?
	What is our solution?	What is our message?
So What	How do we capture their attention?	How will I communicate my message?
Now What	Desired action	What is the resulting action or response to the idea or information?

Takeaways for teachers:

- Identifying an audience should be made explicit in any lesson or project. It gives purpose and meaning to student work, and will instill empathetic thinking, which will improve relationships, collaboration, and communication.

- Identifying content based on audience leads to targeted communication. Brain research tells us that communication is more successful when it begins with the 'big picture' that is supported by detail. Students often start with topics that are too broad, and need help and practice narrowing them to relevant supporting topics. As they concentrate the topic, learning becomes deeper and more meaningful.

- Choosing the right means of communication enhances the message. The proverb "if all you have is a hammer, everything looks like a nail" applies to technology integration. If all you do is write, then every project involves word processing. Conversely, if you do multimedia, then every project is a slide show update! There are so many free communication tools available to students, matching message with medium is not a luxury but a skill.

- What does success look like? Make communication rewarding for students—get them to expect results. Minimally, what is the response your students expect? What is the "totally awesome" response they hope for?

Audience and communication go hand in hand. Technology has exploded previous limits on audience size for your students' work. The greater the size of the audience, the greater the motivation, and the greater the learning. This simple formula is true.

Power of Observation

If my dad said it once he said it a 1000 times, "Think before you talk." As I reflect on communication and audience, I think he meant that I should think about my audience and my observations before I start to communicate. Clearly my need to filter was evident at a young age, but I know I'm not alone.

If observation is a skill in the innovator's DNA, how can we enhance our students' power of observation? This is another complex subject, so let's focus on purposeful observation—knowing our audience, using all our senses, noting what is interesting, and incorporating our observations.

Observing with a purpose requires being present and engaged. What and how much we observe are directly connected to purpose. When a student is simply doing seat time, not much learning or observing goes on. They simply care about what is going on elsewhere. But if students are looking for how they are going to use information in an Innovation Age mindset, they should learn to observe and communicate. What is an unmet need that demands a solution now?

Part of observation requires taking note of where our audience struggles or what they care about. This empathy for the audience helps improve communication— how we want to impact them is foremost. It is reverse mapping with respect to communication, if you will.

Keen observation involves using all the senses. Most people, an estimated 65% (*Mind Tools*, 1988), are visual learners who rely on visual cues to learn and observe. The adage "a picture is worth a thousand words" is only true if the viewer is observant. Sounds are loaded with information if you are observant; background noises, voice quality, music, and volume can all yield vital information to an observant person. Our senses of smell, taste, and touch enrich our observations. My point: students need to sharpen their powers of observation and use all their senses to make the most of each learning experience. It is a preamble to all communication, especially in the Innovation Age.

We are most observant when observing what interests us, often unrelated to work and school. Infusing observations from outside interests adds depth to our projects. That is why companies like Google support "20% time," when employees are encouraged to work on projects of personal interest. The payoff for learning and innovation? Making a habit of mind or metacognition to consciously draw connections between outside interests and projects.

Observation is not only about attention to detail and drawing connections. You know the saying "you can't see the forest for the trees." If we are constantly caught up in details (trees, branches, leaves, etc.) we lose perspective. The power of observation includes the ability to catch the important details and step back to gain a larger perspective. A steady diet of direct instruction turns students into passive learners, not keen, motivated observers. Observation should not be limited to science labs; it must be taught and sharpened for all Innovation Age learners.

Openness

Openness and observation go hand in hand. There is no reason to be observant if you ignore the input. Good communicators are open-minded and invite feedback. It is valuable information. If you ignore the feedback you receive, you limit yourself. Likewise, students need to develop openness and opportunities for feedback from multiple sources, not just their teacher. Technology, especially social media, has made it possible to garner feedback from innumerable sources. The metacognitive lesson here—be open to the observations of others during the communication and learning process.

One-Way, Presentational Communication

Most student projects are one-way and presentational in nature. Slide shows, video, essays, and photos may reflect factual information and observations, but they rarely invite others to interact and engage. A powerful image or video clip can change hearts and minds. They reflect the what and so what of the content area or subject matter they studied. The goal is often to get a good grade rather than see the project's potential to solve unmet needs. They fail to find the relevance of what they just learned or how it has empowered them. Being able to present information is a core skill. Self-expression, in all contexts, is essential. Basic digital skills are building blocks for effective communication, especially if the tools help to craft the message more clearly, succinctly, and memorably.

The most difficult thing for students seems to be creating order out of chaos. They often get overwhelmed by a project's detail, color, and options because they did not start with a message, purpose, and audience. Two examples of how technology can help students create a skeleton structure to map thoughts are the use of styles in word processing and the outline view in slide shows.

EXERCISE
Styles in Word Processing

Sometimes a young writer's best friend is an outline and a few tips on polishing their final copy. Here is a favorite tip I share in my workshops. It helps both teachers and students with writing long documents or reports.

1. **Start with a Simple Structure.** Create a new Google Doc or Microsoft Word document. Type the following words to start:

   Title

   Introduction

   Table of Contents

   Topic 1

   Topic 2

   Topic 3

   Topic 4

   Topic 5

   Conclusion

2. **Use Styles.** Rather than manually formatting each title and heading, we will use Styles to build a structure that we can update easily.

3. **Format the Title.** Single-click somewhere in the title.

Google Docs: Click on the drop-down arrow of the Styles box, which displays "Normal Text" by default, and select Title.

Microsoft Word: From the Home tab, locate the Styles group or from within the document, select from the Style drop-down menu (where the default "Normal" stye is shown). Scroll through until you find the Title style, and click on it.

The great thing about Styles is that they translate universally across applications. They improve navigating through the document if you save it as a PDF. Web page HTML uses Styles too.

4. **Format the Main Headings.** Highlight Topics 1 through 5 and the Conclusion. Use the Style tool again and select the Heading 1 Style.

5. **Reformat the Style.** Chances are the default Heading 1 Style is not what you would have chosen. By choosing Styles, though, you will make it easy to update the document uniformly.

Google Docs: Highlight Topic 1 (triple-click will select the whole paragraph, between two returns) and use the formatting tools to change the font, font size, color and line spacing. Single-click somewhere in the line and click on the drop-down arrow of the Style tool and choose Update Heading 1 to update all of the other headings.

Microsoft Word: Single-click somewhere in the line Topic 1, right-click on the Heading 1 Style, and choose Modify.

Use the dialog box to make your changes. If you use the Format button at the bottom and select Paragraph you can change indents, spacing before and after the heading, and more.

6. **Normal text.** When you hit the Return key after the heading, you will return to Normal text by default. Change the normal text throughout the document by changing some selected text and updating the style as you did in the previous section for Heading 1.

7. **Subtopics.** You get the picture. It works the same for subtopics. You can use and modify Heading 2 and so forth.

8. **Page Breaks.** It is better to insert page breaks instead of returns to force each heading to start at the top of a new page.

   Google Docs: Single-click in front of the heading Topic and hold the Control key while hitting the Return key.

   Microsoft Word (Windows): Single-click in front of the heading Topic 1 and hold the Control key while hitting the Return key.

   Microsoft Word (Mac): Single-click in front of the heading Topic 1.
   Go to the Menu > Insert > Break > Page Break.
   Reinforce the skill and repeat for the remaining headings.

9. **Table of Contents (TOC).** Another benefit of using the Styles tool is that you can build a TOC. Place your insertion point (single-click) right after the heading you created as a placeholder. Hit Return.

   Google Docs: Go to the Menu > Insert > Scroll down to Table of Contents. Update it by changing the headings and hitting Refresh.

   Microsoft Word: Go to the Menu > Insert > Index and Tables > use the dialog box to choose the Table of Contents tab. You can choose a style of TOC and the level of headings that you want to include. Microsoft Word will list the page numbers and allow you to update just the page numbers or the entire table.

Of course this is just a template, and the headings and flow of topics is a lesson in the art of writing. I found that creating an outline that I could modify to fit my ideas was easier than working from a blank slate. I insert and update my TOC frequently to make sure my flow of ideas is clear and that the hierarchy of topics is consistent.

Outline View in PowerPoint

It is so easy to lose one's train of thought when creating a slide show one slide at a time. I love the Outline View in Microsoft PowerPoint because it helps me to stay on topic in a logical manner. (At present, Google Presentation does not include an outline view.)

1. **Outline View.** Launch Microsoft PowerPoint, and click on the Outline View tab at the top of the left navigation area. Click in the Outline View pane. (By default, PowerPoint launches in Slide View.) Making sure that your insertion point is in the Outline View panel, type the word "Title." Hit Return and type the words "Big Picture." Hit Return again.

2. **Demote a Level.** To demote the next line in order to create a bulleted list of the main topics of the slide show, hit the Tab key. Type the words "Idea 1." Hit Return and add five ideas. (Notice that whenever you hit the Return key you will get another line that is the same as the previous level.)

3. **Duplicate the Slide.** Click on the slide icon that you want to duplicate; in this example click on slide #2 in the Outline View. Hit Control+D or go to the Menu > Edit > Duplicate.

4. **Promote the Bullets to Create New Slides.** Click out of the new slide and highlight Ideas 1 through 5. Hold the Shift key and hit the Tab key to promote the bulleted items up a level. (The Shift key is usually used to do the opposite. In this case, the Tab key demoted the line a level, so Shift+Tab will promote the line.)

5. **Remove a Slide.** We no longer need the second Big Picture so click on the slide icon for #3 and hit Delete or Backspace.

6. **Add Detail to the Main Ideas.** Follow the same process by clicking after Idea 1 in slide #2.

   - Hit Return

   - Hit Tab to demote to bullet level

   - Type first detail, hit Return; second detail, hit Return; and so forth

   - Duplicate the slide

   - Promote the bullets into slides

7. **Embellish.** Apply themes, images, and other media. Replace the words, and be concise. The rule of thumb in designing billboards is to use seven words or less. There is nothing more mind-numbing than a presenter who reads every word on a PowerPoint slide.

If PowerPoint is too linear and structured, you can import it into Prezi, SlideRocket, Presentation, or other presentation apps and programs. Remember to keep your purpose in mind: what is your point, what makes it relevant to your audience, and what actions do you want them to take as a result of viewing your slide presentation?

Two-Way, Interactive Communication

Productivity comes from interactivity and
the exchange of ideas and talents.

— Seth Godin, author, entrepreneur, marketer, and public speaker

My concern is that we limit our students' ability to communicate in the Innovation Age if we do not expand their repertoire to include two-way, interactive media. One way to make one-way communication interactive is to add components to invite audiences to respond and participate. For example, students can add action buttons to make PowerPoint presentations interactive or add a survey at the end of a movie to ask viewers to send feedback via a Google Form or survey. Commercial communication has done this on a large scale via social media to keep their audiences engaged. Printed matter usually has links and QR codes to invite audiences to *Act Now*. Students should do the same. If they want their message to be heard amid the media overload they need to be inclusive and aware of their audience.

Interactivity changed the internet from a collection of static web pages to a seemingly limitless instrument of collective intelligence and cloud-based productivity, also known as Web 2.0. Interactivity turned users from passive consumers to participants. Technology users went from recipients of one-way communication to partners in two-way communication and multi-format social media. Social media is responsible for accelerating change, making it possible for game-changers like the Arab Spring of 2011, flash reporting through microblogging, and the success of mobile apps.

Literally every form of media invites user participation through interactivity, but are our students learning to design interactive media to engage their audiences? Shouldn't we enhance our students' communication and innovation skills by infusing student-authored interactive media into the curriculum? This section invites educators to incorporate interactive media into their constructivist strategies by discussing ways to:

- Create "prosumers" of interactive media

- Utilize interactive environments and components

- Select interactive media that support student authoring

- Plan and design interactive media

The definition of *interactive media* evolves over time as available technologies morph with changes in usage and demand. Some definitions refer to interactivity between media or device types. Others focus on the interactivity between users and how the media is used. Interactive media allows users to control their experience to varying degrees, making it possible, for instance, to:

- Play video games

- Shop or learn online

- Apply for jobs

- Vote or participate in surveys

- View details by hovering your mouse over objects

- Comment on stories, products, eateries, events, and venues

- Engage in social networks, post pictures, share links, and write articles of your own

- Map locations and routes

- Work collaboratively in "real time"

The use of interactive media expands exponentially as consumers become users and producers of information. They find new modes of interactivity or create "mashups" that incorporate open-source applets, such as mapping and location-aware applets. For instance, websites like Yelp! customize your experience by combining location awareness apps with shopping and mapping apps. In the context of this book I use *interactive media* to include technology tools that allow users to interact in any way with an application.

Typical use of technology in higher education consists of "one-way technology" (Brown, 2005). Teacher-centered lectures are supported by lecture notes, slide shows, and spreadsheets posted on websites and learning management systems. Interactive media encourages two-way communication where the learner receives feedback, controls the pace and direction of their learning, solves problems of interest, and promotes deeper understanding (Brown, 2005; DeKanter, 2005; Ohl, 2001).

Many universities have started to offer Massive Open Online Courses (MOOC) to expand access to popular courses. MOOCs are a relatively new phenomenon, so conditions and formats between universities vary greatly. Some MOOCs are extensions of face-to-face courses that offer fluid participation by an unlimited number of learners. Other courses require registration for "open participation" and "for credit" with different levels of interactivity depending on enrollment. For potentially thousands of "open," non-paying participants in MOOCs, content delivery is presentational and contact with instructors is not provided. Peer-to-peer discussion and interactivity for "open" students must be accomplished through social media, discussion boards, or microblogs.

Developing "Prosumers"

Helping students to become producing consumers, or "prosumers," benefits them in several ways.

- They learn content more deeply.

- They improve their communication skills to meet current user expectations for media interactivity.

- They enhance their Information and Communication Technology (ICT) skills by using software that allows them to incorporate interactivity.

- They enhance their innovation skills.

As with other constructivist learning strategies, students will learn more deeply when constructing meaning through demonstrated understanding. The use of multimedia dramatically enhances student learning (Evans & Sabry, 2003). Building interactive projects or projects with interactive components requires more complex planning and technical skills than designing presentational projects. The creation of interactive media requires debugging to ensure that each component functions as intended. This ensured repetitive exposure to the content for students in the dissertation study as they designed their own modules and tested other teams' modules. Students displayed intrinsic motivation to go beyond the requirements because they enjoyed experimenting with new technologies during the creation of their eModules. Interactive media is used effectively as an instructional tool through the use of hypermedia, games, simulations, and eLearning environments. Can learners benefit even more by becoming designers of interactive media? The constructivist approach leads us to believe so. Jonassen describes learners as designers in the following way:

> Learners as Designers: The people who learn the most from designing instructional materials are the designers, not the learners for whom the materials are intended. The process of articulating what we know in order to construct a knowledge base forces learners to reflect on what they are studying in new and meaningful ways. The common homily, "the quickest way to learn about something is to have to teach it," explains the effectiveness of Mindtools, because learners are teaching the computer. ...Mindtools often require learners to think harder about the subject matter domain

being studied while generating thoughts that would be impossible without the tool. While they are thinking harder, learners are also thinking more meaningfully as they construct their own realities by designing their own knowledge bases. (Jonassen, Carr, & Yueh, 1998, np)

In his article "Using Cognitive Tools to Represent Problems," Jonassen (2003) advocates the use of computers as a design tool—rather than an instructional tool—for interactive media. This call is echoed by many researchers (Malone, 1980; McLester, 2005; Papert, 1993; Squire, Giovanetto, Devane, & Durga, 2005; Wang, 2006).

Users have come to expect the option for interactivity and hands-on involvement with everything they touch in today's media-rich environment. To be competitive in the Innovation Age, students need to be able to engage their audiences with interactive components or fully interactive modules. The assumption that they are designing for an audience is the basis for empathetic design. It is not just what you have to say, but how effectively you say it. Measures of effectiveness will vary depending on the audience. Successful communication delivers the purpose behind the message.

Authoring interactive media enhances students' technology skills by exposing them to new features of familiar software or challenging them to use new devices, applications, apps, or combinations thereof. Interactive media is best developed in collaboration with others less familiar with the design intentions. Feedback from multiple perspectives is helpful in debugging interactive media.

Students enhance their aptitude for innovation when they author interactive media. Not only does authoring require creativity, students gain practice in the innovation process by developing a prototype, product, or demonstration. They can use the project as an opportunity to exercise innovation skills—associational thinking, questioning, observing, networking, and experimenting (Dyer, Gregersen, & Christensen, 2012).

Interactive Environments

The scale and purpose of the project can indicate whether using interactive environments or adding interactive components will suffice. For instance, students in the dissertation study created eModules to teach their peers about mitosis, the cell cycle, and cancer. To upload these eModules as a self-contained eLearning module students used an authoring tool that fit into a fully interactive environment or LMS. If the peer-teaching modules had been more prototypical, the students could have created slide presentations that linked to a quiz or survey tool.

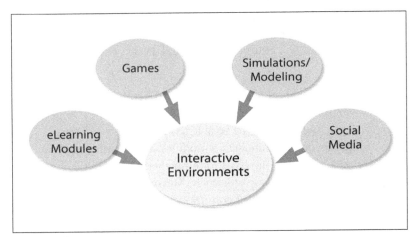

Figure 5.1 | Examples of interactive environments.

Interactive environments include games, simulations and models, eLearning modules, and social media (shown in Figure 5.1).

Let's consider scenarios for using different interactive environments. If students wanted to design a game or app to help others learn, they would need all its elements to be interactive. If students were designing a public awareness campaign for a social or environmental issue, they would have lots of interactive media options if they chose a social media tool. Former eighth graders in my computer class chose to create simulations to demonstrate different strategies to help peers "Just Say No." Students who want to launch a new product might also choose social media. In addition to purpose and scope of the project, teachers should also consider how much additional time the technology might require, how it could be used for other projects or units, and whether the network could accommodate the tools that are selected. Many districts block social media, such as Facebook, but other education-friendly sites are available.

Games

Computer and video games are hypermedia created for entertainment. A game, as defined by Salen and Zimmerman (2004), "is a system in which players engage in an artificial conflict, defined by rules, that results in a quantifiable outcome" (p. 80). Many genres of games exist, making it difficult to pinpoint their educational value (Squire et al., 2005). The popularity of video and computer games is evidenced by multi-billion-dollar sales; ubiquitous formats of video games, computer software, cell phone downloads, handheld games and consoles, and computer downloads; and the reported 2.5-hour daily average 8- to 18-year-olds report spending on computer and video games (Kaiser Family Foundation, 2005). There are calls for the use of video games in education based on the pervasiveness of the media and how it has affected how the "gamer generation" learn and behave (Beck & Wade, 2004; Carstens & Beck, 2005; DeKanter, 2005; Gee, 2003, 2005; Prensky, 2006; Simpson, 2005; Squire et al., 2005). Proponents of this view advocate the inclusion of video games as a teaching tool among other traditional teaching tools (Simpson, 2005).

Characteristics of the gamer generation notwithstanding, Gee (2005) listed some effective learning principles that educational video games incorporate: identity, interaction, production, risk taking, customization, sense of agency or control, well-ordered problems, challenge, "just-in-time" learning, situated meaning, a satisfying degree of frustration, exploration, smart tools and distributed knowledge, cross-functional teams, and the chance to perform before gaining complete competence. Proponents of video games in education say children learn to be collaborative, resourceful, multitasking problem-solvers (Gee, 2003; Prensky, 2006) who gain content knowledge about the context in which games are situated.

> It is paradoxical that many educators and parents still differentiate between a time for learning and a time for play without seeing the vital connection between them.
>
> —Leo Buscaglia

Computer games are not a panacea for engaging learners. Students expect computer games to be of commercial-grade, arcade-type caliber. Those the students typically encounter in school are game-show based, such as the PowerPoint version of "Who Wants to Be a Millionaire" or educational drill-and-practice-type software, often dubbed "edutainment" (Aldrich, 2005). When expectations and results do not align, students are understandably disappointed. Two major studies of game-based learning units found that students struggled to understand both the basic game concepts and the content ideas (Squire et al., 2005). A case study from the College of Computing at Georgia Tech found that games become just another task and cease to be fun when they are assigned as a mandatory school activity (McLester, 2005).

Perhaps expectations of fun and entertainment are unrealistic in the structured environment of school. According to Aldrich (2005) learning is often not fun. Any such expectation may impede simulation development and deployment, not support them. Other researchers disagree with Aldrich and believe that learning should be fun in order to be engaging (Allery, 2004; Barab, Thomas, Dodge, Carteaux, & Tuzun, 2005; Brown, 2005; Cambourne, 2002; Jana, 2005; Wang, 2006; Wenger, 1998). Malone (1980) stated that "Curiosity is the motivation to learn, independent of any goal-seeking or fantasy-fulfillment" (p. 165). He cited Berlyne and Piaget when he posited that computer games evoke a learner's curiosity by providing environments with an optimal level of informational complexity. In his heuristic for making computer games fun, Malone states that these environments should be geared to the current level of the learner's knowledge so they are neither too complicated nor too simple (Malone, 1980).

Many teachers, however, do not see video games as learning tools and are reluctant to devote class time to them (Simpson, 2005). Although the number of educational video games is increasing, they do not address the breadth and depth of the curriculum. Organizations such as the Serious Game Initiative are committed to finding uses for games beyond that of pure entertainment. They seek to go beyond the basics of simple drill and tutorial games and advocate the development of games that encourage "higher-end cognition" (Mangis, 2005).

The broad spectrum of games is matched by the broad range of navigation options. Simple input devices for games use directional keys—Select or Enter, Start, and Option. Computer games often use the entire keyboard, including function keys and key combinations. Most games have menus with options to play in different modes and/or access different player identities. Most games provide a means of saving data so a player can return exactly where they left off, save items they purchased in the game, and save scores. The number of "edutainment" games swelled exponentially with the introduction of iOS and Android games.

Design Considerations

The range of complexity also exists for game authoring options. On the simplest scale, all games involve players producing the scenario through their choices and actions (Gee, 2005). On the other end of the spectrum, authoring commercial grade games is an involved process. Although some researchers use designing computer games as a constructivist tool for student authoring, most educators are put off by the cost of software, learning curve, and development time they require (McLester, 2005; Robertson & Good, 2005; Squire et al., 2005). Games require advanced computer skills for graphics, animation and/or video, artificial intelligence, and dissemination (McLester, 2005).

Malone (1980) suggested that the "computer programming game" is probably the most fun of all.

> In the "computer programming game," there are obvious goals and it is easy to generate more. The "player" gets frequent performance feedback (that is, in fact, often tantalizingly misleading about the nearness of the goal). The game can be played at many different difficulty levels, and there are many levels of goals available, both in terms of the finished product (whether it works, how fast it works, how much space it requires, etc.) and in terms of the process of reaching it (how long it takes to program, etc.). Self-esteem is crucially involved in this game, and there are probably occasional emotional or fantasy aspects involved in controlling so completely, yet often so ineffectively, the behavior of this responsive entity. Finally, the process of debugging a program is perhaps unmatched in its ability to raise expectations about how the program will work, only to have the expectations surprisingly disappointed in ways that reveal the true underlying structure of the program. (Malone, 1980, p. 168)

Fun aside, the popularity of video games has led students to develop one half of their video game literacy—they have learned to "read"—but they have yet to develop the other half of that literacy—learning to write or design. Designing games aligns closely with the tech fluency skills outlined by the National Academy of Sciences (1999) in *Being Fluent with Information Technology*: engaging in sustained reasoning; managing complexity; testing solutions; organizing, navigating and evaluating information; collaborating; and communicating to other audiences (Klopfer & Yoon, 2005).

McLester (2005) listed several principles for successfully designing games: know the objective, decide what skills the game aims to teach, craft an engaging story around the game, make sure content is easy to convey to people, and integrate features that keep players coming back for more. Rouse (2005) provided more specific guidelines. He outlined 12 concrete steps for designing a game: brainstorming, defining the focus, creating the elements of gameplay, utilizing artificial intelligence, crafting the storytelling, designing multiplayer elements, getting the gameplay working, documenting the game development, writing the design document, designing design tools, designing levels of play, and play testing. Rouse emphasized the pre-programming processes of brainstorming and defining the focus, which coincide with the higher-order thinking skills of analysis and problem-solving.

Open-Source and Free Trials for Gaming

Alice. Carnegie Mellon University
www.alice.org

Scratch. MIT Labs free game-making application
http://scratch.mit.edu

Gambit. MIT Labs game development research, sample games
http://gamelab.mit.edu/games/

Bootstrap. Algebraic videogame programming
www.bootstrapworld.org

Sploder. Retro Game Maker, good for beginners
www.sploder.com

Game Maker Studio. Cross-platform app games, good for beginners
www.yoyogames.com/gamemaker/studio

Media Fusion 2. Game and software creation tool
www.clickteam.com/website/world/multimedia-fusion-2

Phrogram. Kid-friendly game-coding application
http://phrogram.com

RPG Maker XP. Role-playing game maker, free trial
www.rpgmakerweb.com

The software options for designing games vary as much as the genres of games. Simpler options for student authoring of games include modifications of commercial games, also known as "mods," simplified game design software, and freeware. Quiz show and Jeopardy-type games can be developed on PowerPoint, and self-correcting Sudoku and crossword puzzles can be created using Excel. Students in the dissertation study had the option to include a game in their eModules by using the simple interactivity options in Captivate 2.

Simulations

Simulations are hands-on training experiences that model an activity or process by mimicking the controls, methods, or consequences of [to] the participant; tutorials are included (Lierman, 1994). Simulations consist of elements that represent objects or situations, and selectively create interactions to enable discovery, experimentation, role modeling, practice, and systems construction to be transferred to the real world (Aldrich, 2005). Simulation games are reality-based games where learning results from the subject matter (Allery, 2004). Simulations are a form of hypermedia that emphasize learning in a realistic setting and may or may not be considered games, depending on whether there are structured rules of play and the intention is entertainment.

Lierman (1994) divided simulations into four categories—psychomotor and perceptual, cognitive-task, communication and coordination, and virtual reality. A flight simulator is an example of a psychomotor and perceptual simulation because it helps participants focus on visual and motor coordination and the sequences involved in performing the task in real-world situations. A stock market game simulates a cognitive task: it helps participants learn the market's underlying rules and principles, though not necessarily real-world situations. Role-playing simulations are examples of communication and coordination simulations— several individuals participate simultaneously, in different roles. Virtual-reality systems try to achieve total-sensory simulation so participants interact with and manipulate the environment electronically.

The complexity of navigation varies among types of simulations and the standard of fidelity or realism designers achieve. A virtual-reality system involves more user controls and simulation elements, which translates to very complex navigation within the simulation. On the other hand, a communication simulation involves a branching dialog with simple navigation.

Simulations are used as a constructivist tool to immerse learners in safe environments to gain experience and construct meaning. The realism of simulations serves to situate the knowledge in a problem and facilitates understanding of the cause-and-effect nature of situations. Game elements are included to replace simulation elements to make the experience [predictable], engaging, and enjoyable (Aldrich, 2005). Simulations are used most effectively when teachers provide students with guidance before and/or after the activity, encourage reflection of their responses, and ask probing questions to delve beyond the simple interactivity (Moreno & Mayer, 2005; Zhu & Baylens, 2005). Simulations are used predominantly as a tool for students to gain hands-on practice and understanding, instead of an authoring tool to present their understanding.

Design Considerations

Are simulations amenable to student authoring? The creation of virtual products and virtual labs is more complex and involves considerable time, technical prowess, and equipment to develop. This translates to costs exceeding $10,000 (Aldrich, 2005). Consider also that when a simulation has been developed, most do not meet all of their goals and require several iterations to make necessary upgrades and modifications (Aldrich, 2005; Lierman, 1994). No matter how effective authoring of immersive virtual environment products can be as student tools, the time constraints and curriculum demands make it prohibitive for content-area teachers to include it as a constructivist tool.

From a constructivist standpoint, the fact that simulations focus on reality serves to emphasize situating the learning. Developing virtual environments and simulations may be too involved for student authoring in content-area classes, but new software makes it possible for them to author branching stories or scenario-type eModules. This type of simulation is similar in nature to the "select your own ending" books that allow users to choose from alternate scenarios.

Aldrich (2005) divided simulations into four basic genres—branching stories, interactive spreadsheets, game-based models, and virtual products and virtual labs—and suggested taking one or more of these genres and customizing or blending the components to fit the learning objectives. Interactive spreadsheets and branching stories fall between. The branching story simulation was the format students in the dissertation study were most likely to use.

Branching stories are simple or complex in structure and fairly rigid in the user experience (Aldrich, 2005). Designers place help or tutoring at different junctures of the branching story because it is easy to pinpoint the learner's location. Branching stories start with an introduction of the goals and overview of the simulation, move on to a simple hands-on demonstration, and advance to more open-ended or challenging situations. Designing the simulation does not follow this order. After the learning objectives and research are complete, designers brainstorm and plan the simulation, insert feedback elements, add engaging game elements, finalize the story, create the first demonstration interaction, and, finally, add the introduction and background content (Aldrich, 2005). Media is inserted at different points of the branching story, and advanced elements such as scoring and timing devices are added to make the simulation more challenging. Branching stories are used alone or as part of a larger simulation or eLearning unit.

Open Source Tools

Insight Maker. Explore interaction between individuals, complex systems
http://insightmaker.com

ASCEND. Carnegie Mellon University mathematical modeling system
http://ascend4.org

SAGE. System for Algebra and Geometry Experimentation
http://sagemath.org

Cafu. 3D environment development for simulations and gaming
www.cafu.de

Geogebra. Multi-platform simulations and interactive media to aid
in understanding algebra and geometry
www.geogebra.org

Branching stories, interactive spreadsheets, and game-based models can be created with relative ease using Microsoft Office applications such as Word, Excel, and PowerPoint. Aldrich (2005) recommended practicing branching stories in PowerPoint. Aldrich also suggests simulations as a way of learning by doing and suggested using a range of toolkits from Microsoft Office applications, Flash, Visual Basic, BASIC PASCAL, C++, and specific programming languages. His rule of thumb is "the easier a toolkit is to use, the less flexible and more genre-specific it is" (p. 318).

eLearning Modules

Summarizing previous definitions for types of interactive media: hypermedia is media that allows users to make selections and choices; games are played for entertainment and have defined rules and quantifiable outcomes; simulations are learning activities designed to mimic real-world experiences. eLearning, as a system of integrated technologies designed to support student learning (Bassoppo-Moyo, 2006), is said to include all of the above. For the purposes of this book, eLearning modules will be defined as self-contained units that integrate the use of a broad range of media (text, images, sound, video, animation, games, simulations, etc.) to support a specific learning goal.

eLearning modules aim to reduce the complex navigation which causes cognitive overload (Cassarino, 2003), while encouraging interactivity. The nature of the interactivity is codified in several ways—by receiver-sender interactions, communication purpose, instructional purpose, activity-based approach, or tool-based approach (Bannan-Ritland, 2002; Hirumi, 2002). When eLearning modules are used as peer-teaching tools, it is important to highlight the instructional purposes of browsing and clicking, branching, and providing practice opportunities, feedback, and coaching.

Cassarino (2003) stated that eLearning is designed as a constructivist learning tool to promote cognitive scaffolding. She argued that providing students with guidance that is mediated by tools in a supportive learning environment is the most efficient instructional model. The instructional system, as a learning tool, must take into account cognitive processing of information, learning tasks, and the learner. Cassarino (2003) stated that an eLearning environment is like a cognitive dashboard, enabling instructional designers to chunk content and design activities for different learning phases. It is not simply a function of information dissemination.

Design Considerations

eLearning content is usually designed by teachers or instructional designers working with subject matter experts (SME). eLearning software and Course Management Systems (CMS) are designed to have a lower learning curve and to be extremely user-friendly for instructors and managers who are not tech-savvy. Interactivity and feedback are integrated into the module without using code or advanced programming. This makes it extremely suitable for student authoring and peer teaching. Additionally, experience with eLearning software is a marketable job skill that students can transfer beyond school.

There appears to be a dearth of literature on the use of student authoring of eModules, but research on peer teaching (DeKanter, 2005; Jonassen et al., 1998; Wang, 2006) indicates that teaching others, regardless of the media used, enhances student learning and retention of content.

There are two main categories of eLearning: asynchronous, self-paced content; and synchronous, virtual classroom environments. This study addresses the former. The general process for creating self-paced eLearning content is similar to designing other simulations. First the learning objectives are established and content is researched. Designers brainstorm the flow of the branching stories, create the dashboard or navigation for the content, collect media files and simulation elements, add feedback and interactive elements, and build the introduction (Aldrich, 2005; Cassarino, 2003). The designer can customize the content while being mindful of information overload (Cassarino, 2003). To support the cognitive scaffolding process, Cassarino recommended that each of the four states of learning, as proposed by Vygotsky (1978), be represented in the navigation— advanced organizers, modeling, exploring, and generating.

Designing eModules involves developing a knowledge base of interrelated and interconnected systems of ideas that are organized as nodes. Nodes of information consist of a page of text, a graphic, sound bytes, video clips, separate documents, or animations. The nodes are accessed through interconnected links (Jonassen et al., 1998). The general process students follow is to a) find information and take notes, b) discuss and coordinate with other members of the team, c) think about the best ways to present their information, d) write their interpretations, and e) link the information nodes.

Open-Source Tools

There are many free tools that allow students to create their own multimedia tutorials and quizzes:

OneNote. www.onenote.com

Quizlet. https://quizlet.com

NearPod. www.nearpod.com

Interactive Components

Interactive media is not an all-or-nothing proposition. It is possible to include interactive elements into mostly static, one-way presentations to allow users to 1) give feedback, 2) control the pacing and sequence of the presentation, 3) fit their preferred learning style, or 4) select elements that provide greater detail. There are an amazing number of authoring options to choose from between installed productivity software, web-based apps, and apps for mobile devices, with more being developed daily. I am focusing on web-based or Web 2.0 tools here because browsers are common to all computing and mobile devices (computers, tablets, smart phones, iOS devices, Android devices, and book readers like Kindle and Nook). To stay abreast of newly developed tools, I suggest doing Google searches from time to time. I also like the Web 2.0 (http://gotoweb20. net) tool directory called GoToWeb 2.0 because it is a filtered database that offers descriptions of sites when you hover over the icons in the results.

Feedback Tools

Ken Blanchard is quoted as saying, "Feedback is the breakfast of champions." This is as true for champions in business as it is for champions of learning and teaching. Yet, how often do we miss the opportunity to get feedback in our communities of learning? Surveys, quizzes, and blogs are good interactive media components to add to any unit, and they do not require a lot of time and effort.

There are many online quiz and survey tools that can be used to create pretests, posttests, opinion surveys, evaluations, and voting. Many LMS or CMS tools include survey tools as part of the package. This facilitates the distribution of the survey or quiz because groups and members are already part of the virtual community.

Kate Lepi's 7 Online Quiz Tools Perfect for the Classroom are 1) Quizlet, 2) Yacapaca, 3) Quia, 4) Google Forms, 5) Pro Profs, 6) Quiz ME Online, and 7) Quiz Star. In general, once you create the quiz online and receive the URL for the quiz, you distribute the link to the class or insert the link on your website or blog.

Online survey tools generally work the same way. The benefit of using a separate tool for surveys is that there is less fear about being graded or judged, whereas quizzes imply a form of assessment. Popular free survey tools recommended by

Richard Byrne (http://tech4teachers.org, 2012) are 1) Kwiqpoll, 2) Micropoll, 3) Flisti, 4) Quiz Snack, 5) Pollmo, 6) Urtak, 7) Obsurvey, 8) Polldaddy, and 9) Kwik Surveys. I would be remiss if I didn't mention Survey Monkey and Baroo.

Some websites are blogs in disguise. For instance, the blog feature that accommodates public comment can be turned on or off on specific pages on my http://alg4innovators.com website as part of the free WordPress installation offered by my hosting service. Most blogging applets allow owners to monitor comments and delete inappropriate blogs. Another way to solicit open-ended feedback on websites is to embed "mailto" or "contact us" links.

Pacing and Sequence

Users can control the pace and sequence of presentations when they are allowed to download and view them on their own. Learners can play audio, video, vodcasts, and podcasts, as many times as they need to if they can access equipment and files. Media players have control buttons to help users navigate through the files.

When users access slide shows and web pages, they can advance content at their own pace using mouse clicks and arrows or scroll bars, respectively. Web pages, including blogs and wikis, generally include navigation bars and menus that allow users to control the sequence of the material they choose to view. Links within the body of pages also give sequencing discretion to users.

Whether you are using PowerPoint, Prezi, SlideRocket, Google Presentations, or Open Office to create slide shows, you can give your users the power to choose their own path of slides, websites, and resources by inserting hyperlinks throughout the presentation. Using web-like navigation in slide presentation gives you the best of both mediums, non-linear navigation and bold visuals and graphics. Posting presentations and assets to the web or in the cloud reduces the number of broken links that often occur with stand-alone presentations.

Learning Style

There are three basic learning styles—visual, auditory, and kinesthetic. Most of us, learners and instructors, are a combination of the three styles. By embedding different kinds of media in our presentations, we provide multiple representations of the information we are trying to communicate. It may not be effective for a visual learner to hear the same thing once or 1000 times; inserting graphic organizers and/or pictures may make a profound difference. Text-heavy web pages or documents often turn off auditory learners, and it may make a world of difference to them to experience a video podcast. We all learn by doing, but doing is absolutely necessary for kinesthetic learners who benefit by physically working through concepts and processes. Once again, offering a choice of media that are inserted into our presentations and documents helps learners to engage and build their understanding.

Detail

Providing users with the ability to access more detail is another effective use of interactivity. An opportunity for more detail encourages buy-in and "just-in-time" learning. Three examples of interactive components that provide more detail are hyperlinks, interactive diagrams, and mashups.

- **Links** to related articles or next steps lead to more learning. Links can be embedded in virtually any kind of document, slide presentation, or web page.

- **Interactive diagrams** provide more detail when the mouse is hovered over different parts of an image. The context of objects and their relationship to other objects is preserved in the static image. Interactive media authoring tools make it easy to create interactive diagrams that display detailed images or definitions when the mouse is hovered over designated objects.

- **Mashups** may be a little tougher for educators to include in their sites, but they're worth looking into. A mashup is creating a new website using components or code from existing sites, such as Paypal and Google maps. Using Javascript or Ajax, depending on the application programming interfaces (API), programmers can add functionality to websites (Schmidt & Kendall, 2007). Mashups can be categorized by type as data types and functions. Useful education apps include metasearch engines, geographic/cartographic data, feed aggregators, translators, and speech processors.

3D Communication through Words, Data, and Graphics

Start-ups and agile project groups that make rapid changes in the Innovation Age need to be able to get their message across quickly and memorably. Effective communicators in small, dynamic groups must be able to communicate via words, data, and graphics. While we used to cater to learning styles and identified ourselves as right-brained or left-brained, those who use just one communication at the expense of others will be at a disadvantage.

One of the most difficult assignments you can give students is to have them design an infographic to get their message across. An infographic can be described as a poster that consists of persuasive words, compelling data, and captivating images. It is telling a story through data. Take a look at some online templates that make it easy to build the infographic once the research is complete.

> **Easel.ly.** Allows you to create and share visual ideas and offers many templates
> http://easel.ly

> **Google Developers.** Offers a gallery of charts that you can use to tell your story
> http://developers.google.com/chart

> **Picktochart.** Offers some templates for free, and expands its offerings
> for paid subscriptions
> http://picktochart.com

> **Infogr.am.** Create a free account as an educator and create charts, maps,
> and video-embedded infographics
> http://infogr.am

Communicating through Words

Because you are reading this book, I do not need to explain the power of words. You probably favor the written word to gain information and to communicate. Being able to communicate in writing is a valuable skill, but poor standardized test scores and rising enrollment in remedial writing classes in college confirm that our students are not as proficient as we would like them to be. There are many writing tools built into applications and apps, as well as vocabulary and language skill-building programs.

Instead of discussing conventional writing tools, I would like to briefly discuss how to communicate through words in less conventional ways. Earlier in this chapter I showed how using styles in word processing or the outline view in PowerPoint can help create order out of chaos. Have you considered using word cloud tools like Wordle and Tagxedo to cut through volumes of words to reveal trends?

If you visit http://wordle.net, you can create a word cloud that shows relative frequency of words in your document by displaying in varying font sizes based on how frequently they appear. For instance, you could copy and paste all of the words of the Declaration of Independence into the Wordle website to see which words appeared most frequently. As you can see from Figure 5.2, the words "laws," "states," and "people" were repeated most often in the document.

Figure 5.2 | Word cloud created for Declaration of Independence

We compiled community feedback from our 40-plus meetings during the Local Control and Accountability Plan (LCAP) process. In addition to carefully analyzing the numerous statements that took more than a ream of paper to print, the Wordle gave us an overview of what people valued.

Words can be used to clarify one's own thoughts and improve metacognition. The individual student journals in the dissertation study helped students to identify goals, accomplishments, and obstacles. They wrote about strategies that worked well so they could reflect on their own actions and impact on improving their processes.

Creating a logo or brand is another way of clarifying purpose and vision. I couldn't quite decide why our 1:1 initiative was so hard to explain succinctly. Maybe it was the quandary that devices in and of themselves were not the solution, yet we were proposing to acquire one internet-connected device per student. Our neighboring district called their program Instructional Innovators, but the name seemed to be disconnected from learning. I wanted the name of our 1:1 initiative to speak to the purpose of the project; we wanted to make a positive impact on student engagement and achievement. We hoped teachers, students, and their parents would achieve that together. The acronym that spoke to purpose was born. We came up with "Learning Environments that Improve Access and Target Needs" in order to inspire, intrigue, instruct, innovate, involve, and invite. Using the Drawing Tools in Microsoft Word helped me clarify the vision and express it succinctly in the logo for Project LEAN In, shown in Figure 5.3.

Figure 5.3 | Project LEAN In Logo

Communicating through Data

Data involves far more than crunching numbers and creating charts. I have encountered so many teachers who are uncomfortable with calculations and spreadsheets that they avoid data as much as possible. Choosing qualitative data instead of quantitative data is not a work-around because qualitative data has to be coded and tabulated.

Good data begins with thinking deeply about what we are trying to measure. This is where communication and critical thinking overlap. How do we measure success? How do we measure improvement? What are reasonable or commonly accepted indicators? How reliable is the data?

In the Summer Technology Academies, we used Google Forms to collect data and analyze responses. Teachers can create self-correcting quizzes as the ticket out the door or warm-ups. Students can create forms to conduct opinion polls and elections, and collect feedback on projects. The possibilities and applications for Google Forms are limited only by your imagination. If you are unfamiliar with Google Forms, the following exercise is good for beginners or as a refresher.

EXERCISE
Creating a Google Form

1. **Log in.** Go to your Google account.

2. **Create a Form.** Click on the red New button at the top of the left navigation bar. Select Google Forms from the drop-down menu. Title your form and choose a theme. Decide who can view your form; if you're using a district domain you can choose to automatically record the user's email address.

3. **File Name.** Name your form by replacing the words Untitled Form at the top; this will double as your file name. Use the textbox entitled Form Description to provide an explanation and directions for completing your form.

4. **Questions.** Create questions by completing the textboxes.

   • **Question Title.** A short description of the item that also becomes the column heading. Keep it short so your columns don't run on unnecessarily.

- **Help Text.** Write out your question clearly.

- **Frequently Used Question Types.** Choose the appropriate question format. Multiple-choice questions produce a single answer. Checkboxes allow the user to choose all that apply. Scale will allow you to create a scale with a descriptor of each extreme. Text allows short answers, while paragraph text allows for longer answers.

- **Required Question.** If you choose this option, the user cannot submit the form without answering this question.

5. **Editing Questions.** The tools at the top right of each question are useful in editing your form. The pencil tool is gray when you are editing that question. You may duplicate the question by clicking the double sheet icon if the next question is very similar. The trashcan icon will delete the question. You can drag and drop questions, using the handle to the left of the item, to change the sequence of the questions.

6. **Collaborating on Forms.** If you are creating the form with others, then you will want to share the editable version of the form. Go to the Menu > File > Add collaborators.

7. **Sharing the Responses.** If you want to share the responses, you must share the response file. Click on the View Responses link near the menu. The first time you create forms using your account, it will ask you where you want to keep your responses. You can choose to automatically create a spreadsheet with the same name as the form. So if you named this form "First Survey" the responses will be stored in a spreadsheet named "First Survey (Responses)." Locate that spreadsheet and share it.

8. **Accepting Responses.** Once you are done with the form, you will want to distribute the URL for the live form. Click on the Send Form button to locate the URL. Copy it to your clipboard. Paste it into the body of an email or document. These URLs are pretty long, so you should use the URL shortener. I like to use http://goo.gl since I am already logged in to my account and I can track how often the shortened URL is used. To shorten the URL, go to http://goo.gl. Paste the URL into the textbox at the top and click on Shorten URL. You'll have a unique six-character address that follows the format http://goo.gl/XXXXXX. If you want to use a QR

code, click on the word Details for the latest entry on your list of URLs and you will go to a page that not only has your unique QR code, but interesting statistics about when and where your code was used on what kind of device.

9. **Analyze the Data.** Go to your drive and locate the corresponding (Responses) form. You can choose to keep it as a Google Spreadsheet or download it as an Excel spreadsheet, PDF, or other file format. Go to File > Download as > select a file format. You can also view a summary of the results. Go to Form > Show summary of responses.

There are a number of websites that provide templates and directions for creating forms. I love Tammy Worcester's tips (www.tammyworcester.com). Try Tip 103: BatchGeo + Google Form, or Tip 81: Self-Checking Quizzes. Google Forms is constantly being updated without notice to users. For instance, you may have noticed that you can insert images and headings into forms. Templates are now customizable with your own graphics and wallpapers.

Advanced form users find Google Forms add-ons and extensions are real time-savers. Look for video tutorials on add-ons, such as FormMule, Choice Eliminator, Value List, and Doc Appender, FormRanger, and FormEmailer.

Communicating through Graphics

I confess that I am a frustrated graphic artist. From the time I started working on my high school yearbook and throughout my college and advertising career, I dabbled in photography, typesetting, layout, animation, and video. I started drawing too late in my academic career, but computers have made it possible for me to work with and learn from graphics. I agree with Walt Disney when he said, "Of all of our inventions for mass communication, pictures still speak the most universally understood language."

I developed an entire 12-hour workshop, "Enhancing Visual Learning through Media and Technology," to help teachers who do not teach computer electives to use readily available apps and web-based tools to harness the power of images. Earlier in this chapter I talked about creating the logo for Project LEAN In using the Drawing Tools in Microsoft Word. I took a screenshot of the finished product using Jing by Techsmith to create a single PNG image file. I encourage you to explore the Drawing Tools using a blank page as your canvas. Google Apps includes a Drawing tool as well, and it is a lot of fun creating an infographic simultaneously as a group.

Autodesk has numerous versions of Pixlr available for free—online at http://pixlr.com, as an iOS or Android app, and as a Google App. Here are the directions for creating a collage using layers and multiple images.

EXERCISE
Directions for Creating a Collage

1. **Create a File.** Launch a browser (Chrome, Firefox, Safari, or Internet Explorer) and go to http://pixlr.com. Use the image editor > create a new file. Select your image size or use the default settings for your first collage.

2. **Add an Image.** Use the Menu within the Pixlr window (not the browser window) and go to File > Open image. Browse the files on your computer to locate the image you want to add. Make sure you have selected the Selection tool (marching ants tool) to select the portion of the picture that you want to add to the collage. Starting from the top left part of the image you want, press and drag out to select the rest of the picture. Note if you want feathered edges, change the feathering to about 20 pixels before you make your selection.

3. **Copy Image** (Control+C or Edit > Copy) to your clipboard. Go to the canvas of your new collage and paste the image (Control+V or Edit > Paste). If

you look at the Layers panel you will see that the image has been pasted on a new layer.

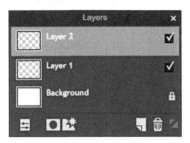

4. **Resize the Image.** Go to Edit > Free transform > use the handle bars (hold shift to keep image in proportion). Enter. Click on the Move tool. Drag the image into place. Using the Layers Panel, move the new layer to the appropriate layer.

5. **Add Images.** Add all the images that you want, following the same process.

6. **Add a Banner.** Add a layer (on the Layers panel, click on the new layer icon, third from the left with the sparkle on it) and move it to the top. Use the shape tool to create a banner as the background for the text. To select a color from the picture, click on the color swatch and when the cursor turns into an eyedropper, click on a spot from the picture.

7. **Enclose the Banner.** Click and drag a rectangle for the banner.

8. **Add Text.** Select the text tool. Use the text tool dialog box to create your text. A new layer is created whenever you click on a non-text layer while the text tool is selected. To edit text, select the correct layer > choose the text tool > when the cursor looks like an insertion tool, click and place the insertion point inside of the text box.

9. **Save Your Collage.** Using the Pixlr Menu, go to File > Save. Use the dialog box to save the file in at least two formats—as a PDX file so you can edit the image again and as a JPG or PNG so you can view the file and insert it into other projects.

There are countless drawing and painting tools for all ages. The important thing is to include graphics as part of your communication repertoire. The world is flat and multilingual in the Innovation Age. Pictures make your message understandable to a broader international audience.

Summary

What   Effective communication skills are essential to meaningful collaboration. One-way communication is entertaining and an important part of self-expression. Two-way communication engages audiences by inviting their feedback, participation, and support. In the Innovation Age, students need to have at least a 3D repertoire of communication skills that lets them express their ideas through words, data, and graphics.

So What   Most student projects consist of one-way, presentational expressions of their research, art, or demonstrations of technology skill. To make our students effective Innovation Age communicators, we need to give them an awareness of audience, fluency with interactive media, and the ability to persuade using 3D communication skills.

Now What   Teachers will include interactive media in their students' repertoire and teach them to communicate more persuasively and critically by using words, data, and graphics.

Up Next...

Creativity

Effective communication and innovation require creative confidence, associational thinking, empathetic thinking, and understanding of the innovation cycle.

CHAPTER 6

Creativity

> Everything is raw material. Everything is relevant. Everything is usable. Everything feeds into my creativity. But without proper preparation, I cannot see it, retain it, and use it.
>
> — Twyla Tharp, dancer and choreographer

Creativity in education is not simply about adding the "A" for art in STEM (Science Technology Engineering and Mathematics) and turning it into STEAM. Creativity must be sprinkled and sparked through every child's educational experience. They must develop the confidence to use their creativity instead of slavishly following rules and directions. The arts are definitely an outlet for creative expression, but creativity, the ability to make new things or think of new ideas, is not limited to the fine arts. Creativity is an important part of innovation, and one of the keys to Innovation Age learning.

Children start out wanting to sing, draw, dance, make music, take pictures, and make things. Along the way, they give up because they cannot carry a tune or dislike their voice quality. They refuse to draw because their pictures don't look realistic or match up to the artwork of their siblings or friends. They give up dancing because they were unable to find a partner, the right style of dance, or venue. They give up on playing an instrument because they don't have rhythm or can't master a brass instrument. Maybe they didn't have access to a camera or took blurry pictures. Some kids were discouraged from taking things apart or making things with discards.

Giving up on a performing art or art does not need to be a lifelong decision. In fact, rediscovering an interest in the arts can be quite exciting. If you are a teacher who wants to encourage creativity and art but feel you lack the aptitude, don't leave it for the art teacher. Join Peter Reynolds and his team at Fablevision for International Dot Day and make your mark by starting with a dot (http://www.thedotclub.org/dotday). Use computer-based drawing tools—I rediscovered my love of art using Photoshop, drawing tools in Microsoft Office, Flash, and recently, the myriad of apps for my iOS and Android devices—to awaken the frustrated artist in you. Dance, draw, sing, build, or shoot pictures because it is fun and you enjoy it. You'll get better with practice, especially if you join others with the same interest.

Tom Kelley, author of *The Art of Innovation,* and his brother David, founder of IDEO and the Hasso Plattner Institute of Design (d.school) at Stanford, say that "Creative confidence is like a muscle—it can be strengthened and nurtured through effort and experience" (Kelley & Kelley, 2013). They say that it is a myth that creativity is a fixed trait, tied to a creative gene. It is time to debunk that myth and trigger the creativity in every student. To do that, we must encourage all teachers to build creative confidence in themselves as well as in their students.

Creativity is probably the most difficult of the 4Cs to teach and measure. In this chapter, we'll explore the following four concepts that ensure that creativity is exercised and strengthened by integrating it with the other Cs—collaboration, communication, and critical thinking:

- A "50 Solutions Mentality"
- Associational Thinking
- Empathetic Thinking
- Innovation Cycle

Having a "50 Solutions Mentality"

"Who knows the answer?"

How many times have you as a teacher asked that question? How many times as a learner have you sought that elusive right answer?

In the information age, it was all about knowing the right answer. High-stakes tests were composed of multiple-choice questions with single correct answers. Millions of Scantron machines were sold to grade similar tests. If there was only one right answer, it was the smart kid who raised a hand to offer it. It was humiliating and embarrassing to give the wrong answer. Too many students disengaged from school because they couldn't produce the right answer often enough.

In the Innovation Age, it is about finding solutions to unmet needs. You have to be able to spot problems and situations that need to be corrected or improved. You need to make mistakes in order to improve. Information is accessible to everyone, so claiming only one right answer is no longer good enough. Does that mean that 2+2 no longer equals 4? Well, in base 4 it would be 10. If you asked students to show their answer, how many variations could they come up with?

Tina Seelig, author of inGenius: A Crash Course on Creativity (2012), introduced me to the concept of looking for 50 solutions when I was enrolled in her massively open online course (MOOC) on Design Thinking. We started by picking someone in our field of work and interviewing them to find out their biggest problems. We were asked to get more detail about their problems to get a better idea of the contributing factors. The assignment followed: we needed to brainstorm 50 solutions to an unresolved problem.

I doggedly tried to come up with 50 solutions, some of which were pretty dubious. I noticed that it was liberating to know I had to come up with so many because I was free to consider them all. I started asking a lot of questions that started with "what if" and "why not" even before I read tips on questioning in The Innovator's DNA (Dyer, et al., 2011). The areas that were seemingly pie-in-the-sky became rich with potential and more fun to pursue. I became intrigued. In a subsequent MOOC, Tina Seelig posted an assignment to find 100 solutions. (I think having a "50 solutions mentality" gets the point across.)

If you've been reading the chapters in order, this quest for 50 ideas may sound familiar. In Chapter 4— Collaboration, I described the Top 10 Research Tips project, which started with giving individuals time to do preliminary work on research tips for their target group, continued by asking them to come together to assemble their 50 tips, distill them to the best 10, and present them in as close to three minutes as possible.

We used Google Presentation to brainstorm, refine, and present our ideas. If this had been a class assignment I would have given students credit for each step in the process so there would be a balance between personal accountability, collaboration, and creative thinking. The research tips in and of themselves were only mildly useful because there is a wealth of research tips on the internet. What participants found more useful was discovering that they were capable of thinking up 50 tips in a short amount of time and how much more creative they felt. Building creative confidence is fun!

Another important by-product of the "50 solutions mentality" is in the group dynamic. This was a group mission to come up with 50 solutions in 15 minutes and no time could be wasted on being judgmental or reticent about sharing.

Associational Thinking

The "50 solutions mentality" is just one way to strengthen associational thinking, one of the five innovation skills found in *The Innovator's DNA* (Dyer et al., 2011.) The first stage of finding 50 solutions may come from random brainstorming. As the lively brainstorming subsides, random thoughts will lead to additional, related ideas. It is not unlike using decoding skills to sound out words with similar letter groups. In math, you look for patterns and apply them to similar problems.

Initially, being creative (random, abstract) and using patterns seems counter-intuitive or contradictory. Others would argue that it is the artful repetition or flow of patterns that add to creativity's appeal.

Innovators develop their associative or associational thinking to be more productive. Dyer, Gregersen, and Christensen offer five tips to strengthen associational thinking: 1) make unusual combinations, 2) take on a different persona, 3) keep a "thinking box" with unusual items, 4) generate metaphors with "what if" starters, and 5) SCAMPER.

1. **New Combinations**. Bringing unusual items or conditions together jars one out of the ordinary or mundane. The contrast can be thought provoking as well as amusing, such as giraffes and baseball.

2. **New Perspective.** Taking on a different persona, whether it is a competitor, target audience, or totally disconnected third party, also forces new thought associations.

3. **Unusual Items.** The "thinking-box" idea is that unrelated items create new associations. Some people like to have rocks or keepsakes in their thinking box. I found a sandscape box in Seattle that shifts and creates colorful new landscapes when I shake the bubbles. It reminds me that shake-ups can create other equally pleasing, unexpected landscapes; I feel free to think "outside the box." Instead of taking a superficial look at the items, think how they work or change.

4. **New Metaphor.** What if innovation was like riding a bicycle? Would it mean that you would recapture the unfettered creativity of a child and recall how to be creative? Does it mean having balance, shifting gears, being willing to fall down and get up again? Just by juxtaposing cycling and innovation, my mind created fresh associations, positive and negative.

5. **SCAMPER.** SCAMPER is a concept from *Thinkertoys: A Handbook of Creative-Thinking Techniques* (Michalko, 2006), an anagram for Substitute, Combine, Adapt, Magnify/Minimize, Put to other uses, Eliminate, Reverse/Rearrange. Although one would probably not apply all of these actions to one project, falling back on one or two SCAMPER verbs helps to break a mental block or solve a problem. What if you used an automatic fish feeder to regulate adding chemicals into a swim spa? Would you have to modify some parts to adapt to the size of the chlorine granules, or make the housing more waterproof?

Lotus Diagram Graphic Organizer

Creativity and critical thinking are closely related. I originally used the Lotus Diagram as a graphic organizer to help create order out of chaos as a final review exercise for implementing the Common Core. As I wrote about associational thinking, I could see how the Lotus Diagram could be used to develop associational thinking and the habit of zooming in and out regularly.

Review and Categorizing Tool

We placed the 4Cs (collaboration, communication, creativity, and critical thinking) in the corners of the "blossom" around the central idea and inserted the infused skills in between (Reading and Writing, Research, Media, and Technology). These eight concepts became the centers of the eight "blossoms" surrounding the central idea/blossom. We used Google Sheets as our tech tool and proceeded to use the Lotus Diagram to review the concepts related to each subtopic. My cheat sheet with the directions follows below. These were the learning outcomes from the workshop session:

> **What.** Explore various graphic organizers that support critical thinking or associational thinking.

> **So What.** Use the Lotus Diagram to review the professional development session on "Using Google Apps for Education to Implement the Common Core" and to develop spreadsheet skills.

> **Now What.** Break the ice for teachers who had never used Google Sheets and encourage them to try it, even just to create a template for the Lotus Diagram.

Associational Thinking Tool

Place the problem in the center of the central blossom. Brainstorm solutions around the central problem. There is room for eight broad solution areas; you don't have to use all of them. Zoom in on specific solution areas by using the surrounding cells to list related, but more detailed solutions. Zoom in and out to different "blossoms" or solution groups, cross-pollinating as you go.

Use the Lotus Diagram to associate technology and communication. The problem can be stated as, "How can technology be leveraged to improve students' communication skills?" Write "Technology and Communication" in the center of the central blossom. Start by taking ideas from the prior chapter on communication and insert ideas around the central idea, such as communicating through word processing, words as graphics, publishing, audio/sound, data and graphs, animation and video, images and infographs, interactive media, and so forth. Each of the ideas becomes the center of a blossom, which in turn sparks project ideas. Using the ideas, teachers can sequence the projects after considering their complexity and the technical expertise they would require. Once again, every space does not need to be used. A richer curriculum may be the product of focusing only on the most promising blossom. The Lotus Diagram helps create order out of chaos and the analysis and prioritization processes.

Obviously, the Lotus Diagram can be created on paper, in Excel, or created in Google Sheets. The advantage of using Google Sheets: people can enter their ideas, and collaborate, simultaneously.

EXERCISE
Lotus Diagram Cheat Sheet and Instructions

The Lotus Diagram graphic organizer, shown below, helps create order out of chaos. Choose a central idea to start, then fill in eight related concepts. There is space for up to eight details that support the related concepts. You don't have to fill in all of the blocks, but you will have up to 62 spaces. These are quick instructions for creating a fillable Lotus Diagram using Google Spreadsheets.

1. **Create and Name Your Document.** From Google Drive, click on the Create button and select Spreadsheet. Click in the top left corner and replace the title Untitled Document with Lotus Diagram Template.

2. **Create the Blocks.** Adjust the height and width:

   - Click on the top left corner to select all cells of the spreadsheet.

   - Hover the cursor over one of the row borders until the cursor looks like a row height adjuster. Drag the border to adjust the height of all cells. Repeat the process if you want to adjust the width of each cell.

3. **Add Borders.** Click in cell A1 and drag across to column one and down to row nine. Click on the border tool and select all borders.

4. **Wrap Text.** While the 81 cells are still highlighted, go to Format > Wrap Text.

5. **Add Color.** Go to E5 and type the words Main Idea as your placeholder. Click in D4, and while holding the Control key click on B2 (this allows you to select non-contiguous cells). Use the Fill tool to make the cells red; follow this process to color pairs of cells.

6. **Insert a Formula.** Click on one of the partner cells and type = and the cell location of its partner. So if B2 will be the same idea as D4, click in B2 and type =D4.

	Collaboration			Research			Communication	
			Collaboration	Research	Communication			
	Media		Media	Main Idea	Technology		Technology	
			Critical Thinking	Reading & Writing	Creativity			
	Critical Thinking			Reading & Writing			Creativity	

The sample above is partially started with the characteristics of Common Core lessons. Teachers were asked to fill in the blossoms around the main ideas as a review. In this case, the tech academy focused on integrating technology into Common Core lessons, so we started with Common Core as the main idea. We anchored the corners with the 4Cs and filled in the other four cells in the central blossom with other characteristics of Common Core lessons. The surrounding blossoms were placeholders for activities and ideas for incorporating and applying those characteristics or skills. Not every cell has to be filled, and it was helpful to see activities in clusters instead of scattered randomly around the document.

Empathetic Thinking

Empathetic thinking is what distinguishes learning in the information age from learning in the Innovation Age. Think about the difference between "Create" (higher-order thinking skills) and "Creativity" (one of the 4C characteristics of Common Core instruction). In the information age, teachers had students create projects to construct meaning. In the Innovation Age, teachers develop creativity in students to empower them to find solutions to unmet needs.

Finding solutions to problems requires understanding the problem and those who will benefit from the solution. Advertising and marketing campaigns begin with identifying and knowing the target demographics; in education we often look at subgroups. In business, users = customers; in education, users = learners. If users are going to be beneficiaries of innovation, innovators must truly understand their users and their needs. They must align output with outcome(s). What is created must address an unmet need, not be just an extension of whimsy, to be a successful innovation. David Kelley calls this creative process, which focuses on user needs, "empathetic design."

To be competitive in the Innovation Age, students need to make an impact on their audiences. This assumes that they are designing for an audience, which is the basis for empathetic design. It's not just what you can create, but its impact. Empathetic design goes beyond tolerance for different perspectives; it capitalizes on multiple perspectives for better, more elegant solutions.

Following are some steps that can help teachers ensure that empathetic thinking is infused throughout the learning process.

- **Begin Projects with Empathetic Thinking.** Focus students on the audience for their projects, and make them aware of empathetic design. Their projects will be more powerful and meaningful as a result.

- **Assess Empathetic Thinking.** Reinforce the importance of empathetic design and "next-steps thinking" by including them in the rubric. After all, what matters is assessed.

- **Formalize Empathetic Thinking.** As students become more aware of audience and the need for empathetic thinking, make learning about the audience a formal step in the project. Think of the empathy map Tom Kelley uses in the design thinking process at d.school (See Chapter 2).

- **Revisions and Iterations.** Focus on the user as adjustments are being made to projects. Revisit user needs as subsequent iterations of the solution emerge.

Design thinking is very similar to empathetic thinking in both theory and practice. Thousands of people have enrolled in free massively open online courses (MOOCs) on different design-thinking courses offered by Stanford University. A design-thinking toolkit is available to help teachers understand the creative process and implement solutions in their classroom, school, and community (www.designthinkingforeducators.com).

Innovation Cycle

Understanding Tarak Modi's Innovation Life Cycle (2012) brings the business and entrepreneurial perspective to creativity through such steps as presenting ideas to stakeholders. Creativity and generating ideas is only part of the cycle. It takes persistence, openness, experimentation, and critical thinking throughout the process. It's also important to note that innovation is a cycle that begins again after implementation, whether it is improving an existing product or bringing something new to the mix.

There is no single magic formula or cycle for innovation. Each designer seems to have a system that works for them. Chris Frink, one of Kelley's partners at IDEO, summarizes his process as Design-Driven Innovation (Kelley, 2013):

1. **Inspiration.** Get your inspiration by going out into the world to seek experiences that spark your imagination.

2. **Synthesis.** Make sense of what was learned in the field and try to find themes, patterns, and meaning in what you observed.

3. **Ideation and Experimentation.** Explore, experiment, and devise multiple solutions. Zero in on the most promising ones and develop them further.

4. **Implementation.** Refine your ideas and map out a road to market.

Summary

What	Creativity can be coaxed or killed.
So What	Teachers can encourage creative confidence by sharing a "50 solutions mentality," associational thinking, and empathetic thinking. Understanding the Innovation Cycle brings the business, entrepreneurial perspective to creativity.
Now What	Students and teachers will be more creative as they seek solutions to unmet needs whether or not they are directly related to core content.

Up Next...

Critical Thinking

Boost innovative thinking by coupling creativity with critical thinking skills. See how questioning, reflection, experimentation, and iterative thinking can spur creativity.

CHAPTER 7

Critical Thinking

5% of the people think; 10% of the people think they think; and the other 85% would rather die than think.

Education is not the learning of facts, but the training of the mind to think.

— Thomas Alva Edison

Both of these quotes are attributed to Thomas Alva Edison. My initial reaction to the first one was to laugh. After reading some responses to the quote, I thought it was a perfect, provocative starting point for discussing critical thinking.

Believe it or not, there is a Critical Thinking Community at www.criticalthinking.org. Its parent foundation provides learning materials for students. Here is part of its definition of critical thinking:

> Critical thinking is the intellectually disciplined process of actively and skillfully conceptualizing, applying, analyzing, synthesizing, and/or evaluating information gathered from, or generated by, observation, experience, reflection, reasoning, or communication, as a guide to belief and action. In its exemplary form, it is based on universal intellectual values that transcend subject matter divisions: clarity, accuracy, precision, consistency, relevance, sound evidence, good reasons, depth, breadth, and fairness.

Dictionary.com has a more concise definition: "disciplined thinking that is clear, rational, open-minded, and informed."

In other words, critical thinking is not just thinking. It involves evaluating received information with an informed, curious, open-minded, rational, reflective, and persistent mindset. Asking the right question is not only integral to critical thinking, it is part of *The Innovator's DNA* (Dyer, Gregersen, & Christensen, 2011). Critical thinking is one of the 4Cs of Common Core instruction, but how does it impact teaching and learning in the Innovation Age? This chapter explores four aspects of this broad question: questioning, reflection and reflexivity, experimentation, and the iterative learning process.

Questioning

If Edison were alive today, I'd ask him how he arrived at his percentages. What was his sample in terms of demographics, size, and time frame? How frequently did he have to observe the person thinking to consider them in the 5%; after all, no one thinks 100% of the time. How would he differentiate between a person who is thinking and a person who thinks she is thinking?

Stepping back, I have to wonder if any of that matters if thinking does not always involve critical thinking.

Every chapter in the book began in my mind with what, so what, And now what, and ends with a summary that distills the main ideas to the same three questions. Coincidentally, *The Innovator's DNA* offers a similar sequence of questions. The authors suggest a series of questions to disrupt the status quo, which I have categorized as follows:

What. Ask lots of "what ifs" to better understand problems: who, what, when, where, why, and how.

So What. Look for causes with a series of questions that start with "what caused...", and search for the ones that had the greatest impact or relevance to the target audience.

Now What. Explore possibilities and gain additional insight by asking "what if..." and "why not?" How can we use the information we uncovered by asking questions and applying them to unmet needs?

In traditional classrooms, the teacher asks the questions and students find the answers. Teachers don't often ask students to come up with more questions. A critical part of metacognition and learning to think critically is to ask questions.

In the dissertation study, students needed to create questions to test the effectiveness of their eModules. This forced them to scrutinize the most important concepts in their narratives, including any common misconceptions and points of confusion. Writing questions or quizzes can be used as an effective form of assessment (Wiliam, 2011).

So how can teachers encourage students to ask thoughtful questions without going mad in the process? Some questions should be directed to teachers for clarification and group discussion. Students should question each other throughout the development of projects: brainstorming, evaluating research, reflecting on their work throughout the process, building in interactivity, and finding solutions outside of the classroom. Students should ask themselves questions and record them in their notebooks, journals, or blogs.

Reflection and Reflexivity

Self-reflection is like looking in the mirror and recording what you see. It is an important part of understanding the learning process and critical thinking. Reflexivity takes reflection to a deeper level. Instead of pondering, "What am I doing?" it asks, "What am I doing in context of the outside/larger world?" When teachers include reflexivity in the critical thinking process it makes students aware of their limited perspective and that it includes biases and limitations. If that helps students to be more open-minded it can also make them empathetic and critical thinkers, and effective collaborators.

Graphic Organizers

Graphic organizers, like the Lotus Blossom in the previous chapter, help students record their ideas in an organized manner, which requires them to analyze and summarize what they've brainstormed, researched, or conceptualized.

When we explored graphic organizers as part of the workshop on Critical Thinking, we used TodaysMeet (www.todaysmeet.com) to collect our resources. TodaysMeet is a free resource and automatically creates transcripts of the chat, which read from top to bottom instead of latest comment on top. In addition to creating class notes, TodaysMeet can be used as a back channel during discussions, or a "parking lot" for issues to reduce interruptions in large meetings. Click on the Room Tools at the bottom of the chat page for transcripts, shortened URLs for the room, and setting the close date. TodaysMeet Teacher Tools offers additional features (for a fee) and a teacher account can be created through your Google Apps for Education account.

A quick search for graphic organizers yields a plethora of results, such as Venn Diagrams, fishbone, sequence organizers, compare and contrast, concept maps and more. Some websites offer free printable graphic organizers; others provide interactive, fillable organizers.

One of my favorite websites for graphic organizers is Holt Interactive Graphic Organizers at http://my.hrw.com/nsmedia/intgos/html/igo.htm. There is a wide variety of fillable graphic organizers sorted into categories, including:

- Generating, Identifying, and Organizing Details

- Determining Main Idea and Drawing Conclusions

- Order and Sequence

- Comparison-Contrast and Cause and Effect

- Process and Cycle Diagrams

- Evaluating and Making Decisions

- Persuasive and Supporting a Position

- Vocabulary

We were sharing our favorites and enjoying the wealth of interactive graphic organizers when a teacher asked about working on them in teams or groups. It's a natural progression from the whole collaboration theme, and it made me think. Was she talking about three students on one computer taking turns, or was she envisioning three students working collaboratively, each with their own computer? These online forms could only be filled out on one computer, which meant someone had to act as the recorder, or they took turns at the computer or tablet.

Collaborative Graphic Organizers

One way to have students work simultaneously on the same graphic organizer is to have them create a graphic organizer using Google Drawing. In the interest of time, teachers can create a template and share it with their students. If the teacher uses Google Classroom he or she could attach a copy to the assignment, automatically create a copy for each student, and opt to have each student's copy automatically shared for comment.

EXERCISE
Flow Chart Diagram Cheat Sheet

1. **Create a Drawing Document.** From Google Drive, click on the New icon in the left and select Google Drawing. Hint: Note your location (check the bread crumb trail above the list of files) before you create your document—you might be in a totally unrelated folder and have a tough time finding it without using the Search Tool.

2. **Create a Heading.** Click on the Textbox icon and press and drag out a text box. Type the elements of the header (e.g, Name and Order) that you want to include. Create a second text box for the title.

3. **Create an Event Box.** Click on the Shape Tool (just to the left of the Text Box tool) and select the rectangle tool; press and drag out a rectangle. Right-click on the rectangle and select Edit text from the menu. Type the words Event 1. Use the text tools to change the font and font size. Use the Alignment tool to adjust the vertical and horizontal placement of text in the rectangle.

4. **Duplicate the Event Box.** Hold the Control key as you drag out a duplicate Event Box to the right of the first one. (Be sure to release the mouse before releasing the Control key.) Repeat the process so you have three boxes next to each other. Move the boxes on either end to the margin.

5. **Alignment.** Hold the Shift key and click on each box so all three are selected. Go to the Menu > choose Arrange > and Align Vertically > Top. This will align the tops of the three Event Boxes. While the three boxes are highlighted, repeat the process of going to the Menu > choose Arrange > and Distribute > horizontally.

6. **Duplicate the Row.** Now that you have three evenly spaced boxes, duplicate the row by holding the Control key and dragging a copy below the original row. Repeat so you have three rows.

7. **Adjust the Boxes.** Select two boxes and delete them. Select the four remaining boxes to the right (either hold the Shift key and select each one, or click on a blank area and capture part of each box). Hold the Shift key

to maintain the vertical or horizontal alignment and drag the boxes in place. Change the number in each Event Box.

8. **Add Arrows.** Click on the Shape Tool > look in the Arrow section and pick the appropriate arrow. Press and drag it out. Use the "handle" to rotate the arrow or resize it as needed. Repeat the steps to create the remaining arrows, or copy/paste arrows to save time.

9. **Share the Document.** Now the flow chart can be shared, printed, or completed collaboratively on multiple devices.

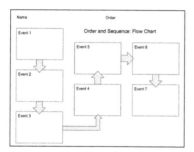

Experimentation

Innovation thrives in an environment that encourages experimentation, yet it is often hampered by a fear of making mistakes or doing things wrong. Innovation and learning are often the result of mistakes and failure. An ineffective adhesive led 3M to produce its ubiquitous Post-it Notes. Dyson built more than 1000 prototypes before coming up with his vacuum cleaner design. Frustrations with movie rental systems led to Netflix. Response analysis helps teachers identify student misconceptions, which represent learning opportunities.

There are so many wonderful quotes about failure, experimentation, and adversity that speak to why we must factor experimentation into innovative learning environments. You might choose one of the following quotations or find your own to display in the classroom or your office for inspiration.

Success is stumbling from failure to failure
with no loss of enthusiasm.

— Winston Churchill

Genius: one percent inspiration,
ninety-nine percent perspiration.

— Thomas Alva Edison

The greatest glory in living lies not in never falling,
but in rising every time we fall.

— Nelson Mandela

A person who never made a mistake
never tried anything new.

— Albert Einstein

There are risks and costs to a program of action. But they are
far less than the long-range risks and cost of comfortable inaction.

— John F. Kennedy

Failure is simply the opportunity to begin again more
intelligently.

— Henry Ford

All the adversity I've had in my life, all my troubles have strengthened me…
You may not realize it when it happens, but a kick in the teeth may be the
best thing in the world for you.

— Walt Disney

You might even solicit quotations from your students based on their own
experiences with experimentation.

A mistake is just a mistake
unless I have a chance to learn from it.

— Justin, sophomore at SHCP

While environments that encourage innovation foster experimentation, understand that there are ways to experiment skillfully. David Kelley (2013) believes that inviting feedback early in the design process produces "enlightened trial and error" and shortens the process.

Innovation should be thought of as an iterative process. Each failure can bring success one step closer if the group learns from its mistakes. Experimentation and metrics for successful iteration should be carefully considered (Modi, 2011). Resilience is another important facet of experimentation that should be part of the organizational framework.

Experimentation can only occur during active learning. If a student tries to simply absorb information, there is no room for experimentation. Teachers are not encouraging experimentation when they are lecturing or demonstrating on the document camera. Experimentation should be part of all learning, not just science.

Innovators improve the effectiveness and quality of their experiments by trying new, unrelated ideas, taking things apart, and building prototypes (Dyer, Gregersen, & Christensen, 2011). Before teachers can effectively encourage the Innovation Age skill of experimentation in students, they need to be avid learners and experimenters themselves. As a teaching professional, are you open to new ideas, trends, or crossing borders? Do you model appropriate experimentation for your students? Deconstructing things helps build insights into how they work and how you can build on existing technologies or practices. Piloting new ideas or creating prototypes can be another way of experimenting.

Iterative Learning Process: Mastery Learning

If experimentation is integral to learning and critical thinking, we are talking about an iterative learning process. It develops grit and persistence and an expectation of continuous improvement. This process is the epitome of Innovation Age learning.

This is the Gamer Generation. They will persist with video games for hours to master intricate levels of play. They are not afraid of the dreaded phrase, "Game Over;" they just start over again and again. They analyze their tactical errors, research cheats and strategies, and spend countless hours in the pursuit of mastery.

Our traditional grading practices do not support an iterative learning process. Grades for worksheets, practice problems, and skills assessments test lower-order thinking skills and learning at the "what" level. Are students given credit for trying over and over and learning from their mistakes? If grades matter the most to students, then how can we encourage iterative learning without affecting their grades?

If the Innovation Age is about what you do with what you know, why doesn't public education support or encourage the fact? Game players are rewarded for their persistence and they can stay on a level for as long as it takes them to pass. Most of our summative assessments do not support mastery; they are designed to measure it and move on.

Summary

What	Critical thinking involves more than thinking. It involves thoughtfulness, open-mindedness, being critical of the status quo, the ability to ask good questions, and a willingness to experiment and persist.
So What	Teachers need to encourage critical thinking and persistence through their instructional and assessment practices.
Now What	Students will become better critical thinkers because of the Innovation Age skills that their teachers develop in them.

Up Next...

Teachers' Innovation Age Challenge

The challenge for Innovation Age teachers is to think and act globally about the changes that need to occur to make their piece of the education mosaic work. Teachers need to assume a leadership role, starting with developing a vision for their school and their district.

PART III

Teachers' Innovation Age Challenge

Without education, your children can never really meet the challenges they will face. So it's very important to give children education and explain that they should play a role for their country.

— Nelson Mandela

How will you use what you've learned about Innovation Age learning?

Part Three is about ensuring that all students have the benefit of Innovation Age learning. Teachers need to pull together so all students have access to technology tools and Innovation Age skills—not just the ones in their class, but every student in their school, district, and state. Help end digital isolation through vision, professional learning, and commitment.

Chapter 8 Vision: Collective Needs and Actions
Look ahead to identify the needs and actions that will lead your school and community to optimize the promise of technology.

Chapter 9 Professional Learning and Leadership
Explore professional learning opportunities that empower teachers to empower students and encourage leadership.

Chapter 10 Ending Digital Isolation
The Innovation Age is a time of rapid change, especially when strong teams are in place. Expand your team. Bolster it with knowledge through collaboration and multiple perspectives.

CHAPTER **8**

Vision: Collective Needs and Actions

The most valuable resource that all teachers have is each other. Without collaboration our growth is limited to our own perspectives.

— Robert John Meehan, author and education leader

Making learning actionable is the biggest difference between the expectations of information-age and Innovation Age learning. If it is not just what teachers know that matters but what they do with that knowledge, then it is vital to have an idea of what we want teachers to do with their learning. If we don't consider this from the very beginning, we will lose an opportunity to fully involve and engage teachers. It will make integrating technology into the curriculum that much more challenging. This chapter is about your district and community acting in unison.

Teachers must think about the collective needs of their school and district, not just their individual classrooms. The purpose is to create a middle ground where the needs of the classroom drive the district's technology vision; in turn, teachers will work with, not around, the district's infrastructure.

The "now what" of this book is to ensure that all students are empowered through Innovation Age learning. This assumes that every student has access to technology to help them learn, that every teacher has access to technology to help them teach, that the technology infrastructure is reliable, and that professional development is in place to help teachers implement technology effectively.

Three superintendents who are part of the Future-Ready Initiative shared their stories about the 1:1 student-to-device ratio, at the 2015 National CUE Conference in Palm Springs, California. Each had a singular journey but a common passion for providing students with technology access, supporting their teachers with professional development, and leading by example in their district's learning community. Their stories provided encouragement and inspiration in unique ways.

> Daryl Adams of Coachella Unified School District works in a district where 99% of students are Hispanic/Latino and 100% qualify for free and reduced lunch. The district adheres to the SAMR model and is working to provide iPads for every student in Grades K–12. The district provides professional development for staff—Superintendent Adams is a believer in lifelong learning, too. He encouraged everyone to "go for it" and work like a technology start-up, where there is true ownership by all.

> Cathy Pierce of Santee School District works in a K–8 district with approximately 75% English Language Learners. Santee started implementing 1:1 iPads in Grades 3–5 in 2014-15, and planned deployment in Grades 6–8 in fall 2015 and K–2 in fall 2016. Superintendent Pierce provides what she calls "loose leadership" with technology integration to set up teachers while keeping students safe. She emphasized communication with stakeholders through a number of channels, including principal meetings with PTAs, superintendent meetings with PTAs, Common Core parent campaigns, and parent iPad institutes.

Duane Colman of Oceanside Unified School District works in a K–12 targeted slow-growth district. The district centers its professional development on the TPACK research and evidence-based model. Coleman calls himself the Chief Learning Officer. His teachers are encouraged to use Design-Thinking proposals to enhance creativity, and he advocates incorporating music, art, and dance into the curriculum to speak to the power of learning.

For my school district to provide at least one device for each student would require major funding. Like so many other districts, resources for tech integration were severely cut during the recession. Each site had at least one computer lab for test-taking, and the testing calendar covered all but 10 or 11 weeks of the school year, depending on the grade level. There were very few computers available for checkout, and most of them were seven to 10 years old. Wireless access was also concentrated around test centers, so teachers could not rely on continuous access. They had to sign up to use the computer lab if all of their students needed computer access

Providing 1:1 device to student access is the goal in the San Lorenzo Unified School District in the San Francisco Bay Area. We are making steady progress toward this goal through a number of serendipitous events and planned action. This chapter was written to share our story in hopes that it helps teachers articulate the problem, brainstorm creative solutions, and fast-track the one that works.

Serendipity

When I accepted the position of director of Educational and Information Technology in January 2014, my predecessors (director of IT and director of Instructional Materials and Educational Technology) had been retired for four and a half years. That's a lifetime when it comes to technology!

I considered myself fortunate. I did not have to deal with the tension between central office and school sites for decision-making power; and school sites were looking for vision and leadership in tech integration and infrastructure. I was also lucky to have the support of Frank Ng, senior network analyst, who ran IT in the interim. He was more than happy and able to partner with me to find solutions that would put technology in the hands of our students. The director of

Elementary Education, Barb DeBarger, who had assumed responsibility for educational technology for two years, in addition to her own duties, welcomed my expertise and generously gave of her time and support staff during the transition.

Serendipity also came in the form of funding. Local Control Federal Funding (LCFF) and the Local Control Accountability Plan (LCAP) brought in much-needed funding—our unduplicated student count hovered around 75% and the community voiced strong support for technology integration. Voucher funds made another $400,000 available to us. There was also local bond money for technology infrastructure and equipment for classroom use.

Vision

The district was in compliance and maintenance mode because of the lack of leadership and funding. The recession hit our high-needs district hard and there were no funds to implement visionary projects. With access to funding I could propose a district context for technology and its potential for students.

 I should have still been in listening mode as I started my third week on the job, but when I was given the chance to engage with middle and high school principals and assistant principals I wanted to offer a game plan. Modeling Martin Luther King's famous "I have a dream" speech, I created a PowerPoint presentation that expressed my dream, which later became our district's dream. The full text of the slide follows.

We Have a Dream…

> … that every student in SlzUSD will get the education they deserve by getting the content knowledge and digital-age skills they need to thrive

> … that every educator in SlzUSD will have the technology and support they need to provide such an education

> … that the proof of that education will be evident

> > … through grades

> > … through scores

> > … through the spark and passion of every student

The Promise of Technology

The dream would remain just that, a dream, without the buy-in of teachers. Our technology department had to earn that buy-in, so I followed the We Have a Dream slides with some solid promises that would make it possible for teachers to trust the infrastructure again. Figure 8.1 shows the Promise of Technology slide, which lays out the goals and promises of the department, renamed Technology Integration Services (TIS). The name change was important—as a department we needed to be mindful that we offer a service, not a regulating force, and unless technology is integrated it is useless.

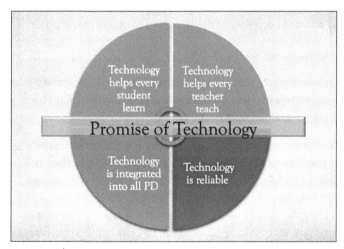

Figure 8.1 | Promise of Technology slide.

It is by design that the top half of the pie represents the theoretical promises of technology: it will help every student learn and it will help every teacher teach. The case that TIS makes to support these promises fills the lower half of the pie: we promised that technology in the district will be reliable and integrated in all professional learning opportunities. We had issues with reliability because we had to make decisions based on budget rather than need. Technology was no longer treated as a stand-alone, but it was not a part of all professional learning because the facilities simply did not exist to support tech integration at all professional development functions. Here are the four promises and a few concrete actions that epitomize them.

Technology Helps Every Student Learn

This promise can be met by achieving the following goals:

- Devices available to support student learning

- Tech integration into Common Core lessons to support content learning

- Tech skills and connectedness for digital-age learning and college/career readiness

- Continuous access to learning environment/tools (Blended Learning)

Devices

Our strategy to ensure that appropriate technologies would be available for student learning in an equitable manner was to use grade-appropriate devices, piggyback on available funding, and take a gradual approach.

In 2015 we began a pilot program introducing Google Play for Education tablets in Grades K–2, comparing the Nexus 7 and Asus Transformers with the clip-in keyboard. Both have the Near Field Communication (NFC) or bump technology that we hope will streamline the deployment process. We had tried iPads and iPad minis but wanted an alternative that was less expensive and easier to manage than the Apple Volume Purchase Plan. For 3–12, we rely heavily on Chromebooks for most student projects. Computer labs and carts of laptops are available for programs that require installed software or larger screens. Our high-end computer electives and school-to-career learning communities have dedicated desktop computers.

Getting to the 1:1 student-to-device ratio based on a reasonable definition (connected to the internet, less than five years old) required consolidating funds from multiple sources. We updated computer labs with desktop or laptop computers with Common Core implementation money to ensure that school sites were ready for standardized testing. We maximized the site allocations from the Classroom Integration portion of the Measure O bond funding. The new purchasing model calls for site tech committees to agree on how they would spend their funds, vendors to refresh their quotes quarterly based on an anticipated bulk order from the district, and purchases being completed as they come in instead of waiting for intermittent orders for bundled purchases. School sites have also purchased technology with Title I and other program funds. Special Education's assistive technology purchases help to improve the 1:1 student to device ratio. The district has also earmarked funds for Project LEAN In, our 1:1 initiative that provides dedicated carts of devices in classrooms of successful teacher applicants.

Common Core Lessons

The devices are just the first step, and they will get as dusty as our mini-labs unless Common Core lessons are fully implemented with meaningful, technology-infused projects. Remember, student achievement is not about exposure to standards-based content—it is about what students do with what they know.

Digital-Age Skills

In addition to foundational content knowledge, students need to be fluent in digital-age skills: collaboration, communication, creativity, and critical thinking. Research, reading, writing, media fluency, and tech ability must be woven into the curriculum to support those digital-age skills. Word processing, presentation, computational, and database training are fundamental to those skills. Digital citizenship and related skills are part and parcel of college and career readiness.

Blended Learning

Continuous access to the learning environment and technology tools is critical to student engagement and achievement. A blended learning environment, which provides face-to-face classroom experience with online access to curriculum and technology tools, offers consistent access for learning and skill building. Our district has a Google Apps for Education (GAFE) domain that provides a cloud-based drive, tools (Docs, Spreadsheet, Presentation, and Forms), and apps that students and teachers can add to improve their productivity. Teachers are excited about using Google Classroom to manage distribution and sharing of documents and assignments. We also use SchoolLoop's gradebook, digital lockers, and domain-limited Loop Mail.

Technology Helps Every Teacher Teach

This promise can be met by achieving the following goals:

- Every teacher has a Teacher Tech Toolkit and the ability to project onto a screen

- Technology supports assessment and record-keeping

- Technology enhances two-way communication between home and school (Parent Involvement)

Teacher Toolkits

Every classroom in the district has either an LCD projector or Interactive Whiteboard. Teacher laptops were cumbersome, slow, and old. Teachers have been working collaboratively to build curriculum and provide feedback for each other in Professional Learning Communities (PLC) for a while now, but their technology had not kept up with that model. The district standard is for each teacher to have a desktop computer, which really doesn't support collaboration when it comes to tech integration. We provided every teacher who attended the Summer Technology Academy with a Teacher Tech Toolkit so they could be fully immersed in and model the 1:1 learning environment. We really didn't want the academies to be mandatory seat time for a laptop provisioning program, so we gave priority to teachers registering in teams of three or more. The toolkits consisted of an Acer TravelMate TMP645 laptop in a padded messenger bag, a CD/DVD burner, a headset with microphone, an 8 GB flash drive, and the invaluable book *Going Places* by Peter and Paul Reynolds, to focus on the heart of Common Core.

Notes regarding the components:

- The Acer TravelMates laptop weighs a little over 3 lbs. and has both the VGA and HDMI ports so there was no need for an adapter to the projector (a cost of $40-49).

- Teachers need a CD/DVD drive to be able to access collateral textbook material and movies. I also wanted them to be able to burn CDs and DVDs to distribute multimedia that they and their students produce. Buying a separate component allowed us to select a very streamlined, lightweight laptop.

- Headsets with microphones were important to the toolkit because we encourage the infusion of multimedia across the curriculum. Whether teachers were viewing video, creating screencasts, soundtracks, or video, they needed a microphone to reduce ambient noise.

- The 8 GB flash drive is probably the cheapest but most appreciated part of the toolkit. Teachers used the flash drives to initially transfer files to their new laptops, but later for gathering and sharing resources.

Assessment and Record-Keeping

Initial funding for laptops and Chromebooks were part of the effort to prepare school sites for Common Core assessment. Our district also administers NWEA tests three times a year. We use Aeries as our student information system to help us with attendance and record-keeping. We also subscribe to Illuminations as our data analysis and teacher-created assessment tool. Our current challenge is to balance the use of technology for instruction with assessment, to be sure that the assessments measure student achievement in a meaningful way.

Parent Involvement

Technology tools are essential to teachers as they partner with parents and guardians to ensure student achievement and engagement. Two-way communication means that teachers and principals not only share information about curriculum and student progress, but that parents and guardians can easily communicate with them as well. We use a combination of technology-based services and face-to-face meetings: SchoolLoop for site and teacher websites, gradebooks and directories for email addresses; Blackboard for attendance and message broadcasting; and district surveys. Tech events for parents have been included in the revised technology plan.

Technology Is Reliable

This promise can be met if:

- Network access is robust

- Devices are managed efficiently

- Tech support is timely (<36 hrs)

- Onsite tech coordination and teacher support is equitable

Network Access

The district purchases its high-speed internet service from the Alameda County Office of Education. The county provides filtering and firewall services as well. The reliability issue for us lay in the wireless access network. Before an upgrade last summer we were using only 10% of the bandwidth, yet the wireless network started dropping users when 20 or so users were on the same access point. Now that the wireless access points have been replaced, teachers are enjoying robust network access.

Device Management

The more we can manage our devices remotely, the more efficient we can be. Our laptops and tablets (iOS and Android) are managed through the Meraki MDM. (Instead of using a dedicated Mac computer to clone a cart of iPads, we can push paid and free apps out wirelessly through Meraki.) The GAFE domain allows us to manage users and site domains wirelessly, as well as to push out apps based on organizational units. For example, we can turn on Gmail for all students at a single high school and push out Snagit for Chrome through the management console.

Tech Support

The average response time for help tickets was 96 hours. As a former teacher, 96 hours was a lifetime to me, so our current goal is 24 hours, not to exceed 36 hours. Three changes helped to decrease the response time: 1) techs work together to share the load now that they are all union workers, 2) we have a full complement of techs on staff, and 3) we are streamlining communication by rethinking our use of HelpStar. Teachers can get the fastest support by using the online form to report issues. This gives techs more information from the get-go and it makes it easier for them to share the load. Anyone in the district can send an email to HelpStar, but they risk a longer correspondence if the tech needs further information. We also have a phone number for the help desk, but we like to reserve it for emergencies. Technicians focus more on network-based and hardware/software issues.

Onsite Teacher Support

We have a staff of Computer Media Specialists (CMS) whose primary role is to support teachers in their classroom or computer lab so they can focus on teaching instead of troubleshooting. As budgets were cut deeper and deeper, CMS hours were cut accordingly. Through LCAP funding, the district increased CMS support based on the unduplicated student count. School sites had the option to supplement their hours with site-based program funds. CMS are a teacher's first point of contact. If the issue requires more than two minutes to resolve, a CMS can advise or help the teacher submit a HelpStar request. Obviously, there is overlap in the work of the CMS and techs, so we encourage teamwork and common training.

Technology Is Integrated into All Professional Development

This promise can be met by if technology is:

- Available at multiple times and venues

- Included when new devices are delivered

- Resources are accessible online

Multiple Times and Venues

The next chapter is about the plethora of professional learning opportunities available to teachers. I suggest we develop workshops based on themes and offer them multiple times, inviting principals to host the workshops at their site. This makes them open to all, reduces the preparation time for presenters, and makes it convenient to teachers at multiple school sites.

New Devices

We always make an orientation training part of the new device delivery process. For instance, whenever Chromebooks are delivered to a site, all interested teachers are invited to the training. Some principals make it a part of faculty meetings so the workshop will not have to be repeated as more devices are purchased and access is expanded to more teachers. Proactive teachers are not burdened with training teachers who missed the initial orientation.

Resources Online

This is definitely an area of growth for me. I started a website using Google Sites for the Summer Tech Academies, but I have yet to complete it. The plan is to eventually strengthen the TIS website to make resources for all workshops available to all teachers.

Comprehensive Technology Plan

There is no convenient time to write a comprehensive technology plan, and it is amazing how quickly they come due again. If your district believes writing a tech plan is a valuable process for communication and reflection, it will be time well spent. At the time of this writing we are in the process of updating our tech plan, and as director I am grateful for the time and wise insights that my committee has shared. This is our opportunity to put the promise into practice with a three-year plan, informed by technology proficiency surveys from teachers, administrators, and classified staff.

The California Department of Education (CDE) no longer funds the evaluation of tech plans and now uses a more simplified, five-section format as of fall 2014. The sections are:

1. Background: plans guide the use of ed tech over the next three years.

    a. Brief overview of the local educational agency (LEA), location, and demographics

    b. Description of how a variety of stakeholders within the LEA and community-at-large participated in the writing of the plan

    c. Summary of relevant research that supports the plan's curricular and professional learning goals

2. Curriculum: clear goals and realistic strategy for using telecommunications and technology to improve education services.

    a. Teacher access and use of digital tools

    b. Student access and use of digital tools, including the LEA's replacement policy and equitable use for all students

    c. Goals and implementation plan, with annual activities for using technology to improve teaching and learning, and a funding plan for the activities

    d. Goals and implementation plan for how and when students will acquire the tech skills and information literacy skills needed for college and career readiness

    e. Goals and implementation plan to address internet safety and appropriate and ethical use of technology

3. Professional development.

    a. Summary of teachers' and administrators' proficiency and their needs for professional development

    b. Goals and implementation plan for providing professional learning opportunities

4. Infrastructure, hardware, technical support, software, and asset management.

    a. Description of existing hardware, internet access, electronic learning resources, technical support, and asset management in place to support curriculum and professional development

    b. Description of needs—hardware, electronic learning resources, networking, telecommunications infrastructure, physical plant modifications, technical support, and asset management—to support curriculum and professional development

5. Monitoring and evaluation.

    a. Description of the process for evaluating overall progress and impact on teaching and learning

    b. Description of the schedule for evaluating the effect of plan implementation, including the process and frequency of communicating evaluation results to stakeholders

I have had the honor of serving as tech plan coordinator, and want to share a few tips I picked up during my work.

I like to start the tech plan writing process with section descriptions, stakeholders, monitoring and evaluation processes, and research so there is a good framework to work from. It also gives the committee quick "wins" and a fast start to writing the plan.

We use Google Forms to create separate but similar tech proficiency surveys for teachers, administrators, and classified staff. The survey is anonymous, but identified by site so the information is useful to site tech teams, and takes fewer than 10 minutes to complete. We improved the survey by listing example apps and applications for the different skills. For example, the skill-based Q7 asks the survey taker to rate their skill level in presentation software (e.g. PowerPoint, Google Presentation, Prezi), from Beginning: limited awareness of how to use presentation software, to Advanced: good presentation software skills, creates presentations regularly, able to help students and colleagues in this area.

We are grateful to the Los Angeles County Office of Education for developing and making available the Tech Plan Builder. This tool makes it possible for tech plan committees to write the plan component by component with the assistance of built-in guidelines, formatting tools, and the ability to export the entire plan as a Microsoft Word file.

Fast-Tracking Implementation

There are three key things that teachers can do to fast-track the implementation of their plan and harness technology for learning and teaching: 1) work as a team, 2) stay involved in the planning process, and 3) take a leadership role.

Work as a Team

When I was interim director in St. Helena, a 1:1 student-to-Chromebook pilot program was in the works for every fifth, sixth, and ninth grader. Teachers had been working as grade level teams, so it made sense to overlay the pilot program based on grade levels instead of individual teachers at various grade levels. Regardless of their comfort level with technology when teachers started the pilot program, they ended up as strong supporters of 1:1. They focused on what their students could do with technology instead of waiting until they cemented their technology skills. (The complete evaluation of the Chromebook pilot program is posted on the St. Helena Unified School District website)

The school sites that took the grade level team approach in San Lorenzo are moving ahead faster than the ones that concentrated resources on individual teachers, teachers who have to sign up for mobile labs, or teachers who use mini-labs in their classrooms. It takes consistent use of technology for students to develop 4Cs Innovation Age skills.

Stay Involved

Don't pass up any opportunities to share your feedback or participate in professional development. Here are some different ways to stay involved:

- Join your site tech committee

- Make a "Tech Tip" moment a daily practice—either share a tip or ask for one

- Participate in tech surveys

- Let your needs be known, but keep an open mind

- Take advantage of online resources and interest groups

- Advocate for your students and share their feedback with your colleagues and district leadership

You get the picture. Whether you're a newbie, making up for lost time, a tech-savvy leader, or somewhere in between, you are not alone. Your involvement means your stakeholder group is represented.

Leadership

Everyone has something to offer as a leader.

We have an Ed Tech Advisory Committee in San Lorenzo that meets once a month. It is important to have someone at each site participating in the decision-making process and bringing back first-hand information. You don't have to be extremely tech-savvy to represent your site.

To build capacity I have recruited tech-savvy teachers to be part of my "TSA by Committee (where TSA means Teachers on Special Assignment) group to provide workshops at multiple venues. Teachers give while they get. Teachers who give workshops gain experience and get a deeper understanding for the topic, and they build their resume for next steps.

Build your team to build critical mass. Lead and learn smart!

Summary

What   Students and teachers need consistent access to technology in order to fully implement Common Core content and infuse digital-age skills.

So What   Teachers are aware of solutions to some of the challenges they face as they integrate technology into their blended classrooms.

Now What Teachers can offer solutions to fast-track consistent and equitable access to technology to improve student learning and achievement.

Up Next...

Professional Learning and Leadership

Professional development and teacher leadership are critical to students realizing the promise of technology. Explore some opportunities and strategies for spiraling upward toward leadership.

CHAPTER 9

Professional Learning and Leadership

If you have a passion for learning, it will become
the drive for everything you do in the classroom.

— Krissy Venosdale, Lower School Innovation Coordinator
at The Kinkaid School

Professional learning in the Innovation Age needs to
mirror what our students need to learn. It needs to
be about and model collaboration, communication,
creativity, and critical thinking in a 1:1 blended learning
environment. Collaborative professional learning requires
individual and group commitment, planning, and shared
leadership. Communication is critical. Creativity makes
limited budgets go farther. Critical thinking before,
during, and after professional development makes the
learning stick and spread. My point: the 4Cs are the heart
and soul of Common Core; and they must permeate
professional learning.

Pulling together applies to professional learning too. If each teacher brings their passion for learning, it can ignite the passion of the entire staff, possibly the whole district. That is what I observe in my district as administrators try to keep up with the thirst for learning expressed by a critical mass of teachers. Late adopters are asking to be caught up. Tech-savvy teachers are embracing the new collaborative technology model. Administrators at the site and district level seek to optimize collaborative technology to be more transparent and efficient. Support staff wants to do the same. It is contagious and exhilarating!

It has also been an upward spiral. Upgrades to the infrastructure and improved access to mobile technology have piqued interest in technology integration. Implementation of the Common Core, community support, and increased interest in technology integration have increased demand for professional development. Since few teachers want to be left out of the new technology movement, there is increasing pressure to provide more tech devices and training.

How is tech professional learning in the Innovation Age different from tech professional development in the information age? In so many ways we had to stop counting. It is like a 24/7 market with miles of merchandise. Just as shoppers from all walks of life get in line, teachers can proceed to the line with their teams or shop ad hoc with people with similar tastes or interests. You get the idea. The choices are endless, and strategic consumption may be in order.

Collaboration

Dining with friends and family is generally more enjoyable than eating alone. Likewise, participating in professional learning as a community is not only more enjoyable, it is also more effective. If you are already planning curriculum as a group it does not put a burden on the tech-savvy to come back and teach others. Teachers can learn and create curriculum together. Multiple perspectives are exchanged and included, and you preclude the need to solicit teacher buy-in at a grade level meeting days, weeks, or months later.

The collaborative nature of Google Apps for Education (GAFE) has been instrumental in creating district-wide momentum for professional learning. When 254 Chromebooks were purchased for Common Core testing in my district, it forced the district to create a GAFE domain (unless it wanted to use them exclusively for testing). A Chromebook is not much more than a Chrome browser (a type of app that gets users on the internet) with some memory in a case. Online testing on a Chromebook means accessing the test app before logging in, which puts the Chromebook in kiosk mode, requiring a restart before any other app can be accessed.

When the district domain was created, we used Active Directory to generate an account for every student in Grades 2–12 and all staff members. We eventually turned on Gmail for all staff and reconfigured the organizational units so that Gmail for students could be a site-specific decision. We chose not to import the passwords from Active Directory and opted instead to force a password change using Google's recommendation to use eight or more characters, including at least one upper case, one lower case, a symbol, and a number.

The first wave of GAFE users were the teachers whose sites had purchased Chromebooks. The next came when the supplemental summer school program for elementary students needed to borrow Chromebooks to supplement student access, and summer school teachers received training in GAFE. The fact that our at-risk summer school students were excited about using Chromebooks and could remember their passwords was encouraging to staff.

The third wave of GAFE users were the 130 teachers and Teachers on Special Assignment (TSA) who participated in the Summer Tech Academies. We conducted a pilot program for the TSAs prior to the three cohorts of Summer Tech Academies that ran for two weeks in June and a week in August. The Summer Tech Academies were so popular that the district decided to fund 70 more teachers in the encore workshop that fall. Scheduling conflicts, rather than a lack of funding, is the reason only 70 teachers were accommodated in the fall. (Details about the tech academies will follow in this chapter.)

There are not enough members in the Educational Leadership Team (ELT) to call them a wave, but they received their toolkits and initial GAFE training just prior to the TSA pilot program. I am a member of the ELT, so our plan was to start with two hours of training followed by supplemental training as learning opportunities presented themselves. We often shared brief "just-in-time" tech tips in the course of collaborating in the GAFE domain. As we experienced how time-saving and efficient shared folders and documents could be, we decided that all administrators should be afforded the same tools and training. Administrators got an intensive 90-minute orientation to the toolkit and GAFE with the understanding that more training would be offered as we progressed through the year and the 4Cs of Common Core.

Other leadership teams that received GAFE training include the directors of Business Services, the three union presidents and the superintendent, the clerical support staff of Educational Services, and the board of trustees. A handful of classified staff attended a workshop, "Helping Students with Chromebooks," over the summer.

Educators are not waiting for formal workshops on GAFE. Some have taken the Google certification on their own. Teachers are promoting GAFE accounts to their students and their colleagues. Each school that orders Chromebooks for the first time continues to receive the orientation training upon delivery of their devices.

So many teachers and tech leaders have expressed interest in what we've done and plan to do with tech professional development that I would like to offer more detail at this point. Tailor these ideas to meet your own needs; they are offered as a starting point and food for thought.

Technology Academies

The Summer Technology Academy consisted of two workshops—"Using Google Apps for Education to Implement the Common Core" and "Enhancing Visual Learning through Media and Technology." All but 35 of the participants took the first workshop; the rest took just the second one. The fall encores focused on "Using GAFE to Implement the Common Core," with one session for elementary teachers and the other for middle and high school teachers. As mentioned in the previous chapter, the Summer Tech Academies were designed to plant the seed for 1:1 device to user learning environments so each participant received a Teacher Tech Toolkit. Additionally, we wanted the workshop to be the starting point, not a self-contained training, for collaboration so teacher teams had preference if they registered within the first 10 days. Single teachers were taken on a first-come-first-served basis after teams were accommodated.

The Summer Tech Academies were scheduled from 9:00 a.m.-12:00 p.m., Monday through Thursday, with an expectation that teachers would spend a couple of hours a day to practice and apply what they learned. We provided lunch and made a space for "open lab," where teachers could get one-on-one help on anything they wanted to work on. Many teams took the opportunity to continue to work collaboratively to build curriculum. In addition to the Tech Toolkits, teachers were paid for the 12 hours of the workshop. Because Google considers curriculum-building the intermediate level of GAFE, we paid teachers $100 for completing the free Google Basics certification before the workshop began. This helped reduce the disparity between tech expertise and its burden on tech-savvy teachers. One hundred thirty (roughly 20% of the district) classroom teachers and TSAs participated in the Summer Tech Academies.

"Using Google Apps for Education to Implement the Common Core" was repeated at Fall Tech Academies for an additional 70 teachers. Two academies were originally scheduled for the first Friday and Saturday of November and December, but due to the extreme shortage of substitute teachers the Friday session had to be modified so teachers were put in smaller groups and divided into a Tuesday, Wednesday, or Thursday all-day session prior to Saturday's session. Although this format didn't allow for as much collaborative practicum, it offered teachers a chance to participate in an academy and get a toolkit without waiting for summer. Fall Tech Academies prepared more teachers to engage in Project LEAN In at the next level of professional learning and dedicated access to devices.

Using Google Apps for Education to Implement the Common Core

Although collaboration, communication, creativity, and critical thinking cannot be isolated, we tried to focus on each of them through concrete lessons that could be applied to the classroom. As difficult as it is to take the focus away from the toolkit and into tech implementation, we had to do a toolkit quick start to get that out of the way. We anticipated that step, and advise you to include it in your plan of action.

We opened the doors 30 minutes early on Monday so we would not lose any workshop time to toolkit distribution. (Some teachers needed to turn in old laptops so we had the paperwork ready.) The laptop specialist, office clerk, and one

IT technician were on hand to make sure everyone could connect wirelessly and that we could troubleshoot any problem laptops.

Each teacher received a color-coded manila folder containing their laptop checkout sheet, a set of six labels (two rows of address labels that included their name, district, and item), the Toolkit Quick Start guide, the GAFE Quick Start Guide, a stipend form for completing Google Basics before the workshop, and the user guides for the laptops. We went through each item in the toolkit so every teacher understood its purpose, had a chance to label them, and, most importantly, removed the dreaded packaging! Table 9.1 shows the agendas for the four-day workshop. The idea was to provide exposure and basic content and allow as much time as possible for teachers to apply it in their own classroom or lessons. Step-by-step instructions for most of these exercises can be found in Chapters 4–7.

Table 9.1 | Agendas for Using GAFE to Implement the Common Core

Focus	Agenda
	Day 1
1. Characteristics of Common Core Instruction and How Teacher Tech Toolkits Model 1:1	Start with the heart. Read *Going Places*, by Peter and Paul Reynolds, to understand why the 4Cs and going above and beyond the standards is important.
	Introduce the 4Cs through the agenda: collaboration, communication, creativity, and critical thinking. Infuse the skills of reading and writing across the curriculum, research, media, and tech fluency.
	Introduce the elements of the Teacher Tech Toolkits.
2. Collaboration in Class	Introduce the district GAFE
	Working with shared folders and docs
	• Setting up sharing protocols and conventions
	• Creating shared documents (Notes)

Focus	Agenda
	Day 2
1. Collaboration in Class (continued)	Data-Mining Activity: Top 10 Research Tips Using Collaboration and Presentation 1. Create a new Presentation document and title it "Top 10 Research Tips for (Target Audience)." Do some quick research so you have ideas to bring to the table (:10) 2. In your group, brainstorm 50 tips using one slide per idea (:20) 3. Refine your tips as a group. Strategies include voting using shapes; discussion, grouping ideas, and synthesizing them (:15) 4. Make a copy of your group's tips and move it to your My Drive (:05) 5. Present your tips as a group (3 mins per group)
2. Collaboration beyond Class	Create a Virtual Classroom or Office Using Google Sites. (Skills demonstration involved creating a sample Common Core website or student ePortfolio. We created a home page and a page for each of the 4Cs.) 1. Think about your audience and sketch out a site map (:05) 2. Check out other sites for ideas (:10) 3. Create a page for each section and start writing (:30) 4. Apply themes, add images, and explore templates
3. Collaboration beyond School	Create a Resources Page Using Your Enhanced Tech Research Skills. Topics that go beyond school include: • Technology tools • Professional learning network • Content area resources • Global experts • Peer networks • Parent connection

Table continued from previous page

Focus	Agenda
Day 3	
1. Communication through Words	Writing to clarify thinking
	Using Styles in Word and docs
	Using Wordle and Tagxedo
2. Communication through Data	Creating a form to get data
	Publishing the form and soliciting responses
	Analyzing responses
	Using the spreadsheet tool
3. Communication through Graphics	Screencasting with Jing or Snagit for Chrome
	Using drawing tools to create a graphic representation
	Big project: create an infographic
Day 4	
1. Critical Thinking	Graphic Organizers. Search for graphic organizers that are appropriate for your students. Record your findings on our TodaysMeet page. (Compare data-mining using a chart with transcript versus a shared document.)
	Create your own iterative learning lesson plan
	Create your own iterative learning rubric
2. Creativity	Discussion: innovation and empathetic thinking
	Discuss associational thinking and use the Lotus Blossom (See Chapter 6) to brainstorm as an associational thinking organizer
	Make your own Lotus Blossom template using Google Sheets
3. Now What?	50 Ways to Leave Your Workshop
	• Use your Lotus Blossom graphic organization to recap what you've learned about the Common Core and how you can apply it to your classroom
	• Map your next steps
	• Complete the workshop evaluation

Enhancing Visual Learning through Media and Technology

More than 65% of our students are visual learners, yet much of the content is delivered through lecture or didactically. The purpose of this workshop was to help teachers dive more deeply into multimedia and incorporate more of it in their instruction.

This workshop was structured just like the "Using GAFE to Implement the Common Core" workshop in terms of hours, compensation, and toolkit. Several teachers attended both sessions.

Table 9.2 lists the agendas for the four days.

Table 9.2 | Agendas for Enhancing Visual Learning through Media and Technology

Day	Agenda
Day 1 Toolkit, Gathering Images, Editing Images	Toolkit quick start Gathering images. Free sources such as Tech4Learning, Library of Congress, Creative Commons Screencasting with Jing: images, video, video screencasting Using Pixlr to edit the rickshaw driver (using the cropping tool, cloning tool to remove distractions, adding a text layer, using the eyedropper tool to select colors that are already part of the palette, adding layer effects)
Day 2 Slides and Sounds	Use PowerPoint or Presentation and screen capture to create images for the video Use Audacity (freeware) to create narration and/or edit sounds
Day 3 Video	Put your components together to create a video. Use MovieMaker on your Windows laptop to edit your video Add an interactive component by creating a feedback survey and including the QR code and/or link to submit a review
Day 4 Video, Publishing, and Screening	Further work on the video Discuss how to publish videos online on websites such as YouTube, Teacher Tube, or Vimeo Screening of videos Workshop Evaluation

Google Classroom

Google Classroom made its debut in mid-June 2014. This free Learning Management System (LMS) allows teachers to manage class assignments through a virtual classroom at http://classroom.google.com. Students can be added manually or given a code to join a class. Teachers can add attachments to assignments, which can be uploaded from their computers or Google Drive. They can choose to automatically create copies for each student that adds their names to their files and shares a copy with the teacher.

Students' work appears in folders by assignment and can be graded in Google Classroom. For instance, a teacher creates a class called "Collaboration 101" and assigns "Essay 1" via a handout/template she distributes through Google Classroom. By looking in her "My Drive" for a titled classroom she will find a new folder titled "Essay 1." Within that folder is a document for each student enrolled in the class, with their name embedded in the file name. When the student submits the assignment he or she will no longer be able to edit their assignment.

Integrating Technology to Implement the Common Core

By adjusting professional development to rapidly changing technologies, we can stay current with available devices, apps, and applications. Teachers at my district were given a choice between Google Classroom and OneNote Class to organize assignments for and from students.

Teachers need to understand Google Apps for Education (GAFE) because of the dominance of Chromebooks in the district. GAFE offers a range of tools, starting with Google Forms which Microsoft Office 365 does not offer to date. Conversely, Office 365 addresses several issues related to document compatibility that GAFE only touches on and offers a more curriculum-friendly virtual classroom organizer in OneNote Class.

Believe it or not, the greatest challenge for students and staff has been logging in and creating multiple versions of the Microsoft Office documents uploaded in the Drive. Sure, Word documents can be opened with Google Docs but the formatting sometimes suffers and users are unfamiliar with the tools. Teachers who prefer GAFE should continue to use it. Our district added, not supplanted, student and teacher options by deploying Office 365. We believe it will be useful for students and staff to have familiar applications (Word, Excel and PowerPoint) in an online, collaborative format through OneDrive. Our licensing also allows families and staff to install the latest versions of Office while they are enrolled in or employed by the district. Another important feature is that OneNote Class allows teachers to organize lessons and units in folios and then view and provide feedback on student work in one convenient file, which can be edited online and offline because files sync when a network becomes available again. This is good for our families that do not have internet access at home.

The list of tech professional development offerings for summer 2015 included two Tech Academies (includes toolkits), a FEAST (Fun Engaging Accessible Summer Tech) mini-conference, GAFE II for previous Tech Academy attendees, and "Using Office 365 as an Instructional and Learning Tool."

Project LEAN In

I designed Project LEAN In to give teachers who participated in the summer and fall technology academies a way to integrate technology on a consistent basis. Our neighbor to the north, San Leandro Unified School District, developed a 1:1 program called "Instructional Innovators;" my superintendent wanted our students and teachers to have the same opportunity. With the extensive testing schedule, teachers could not rely on access to the computer lab or shared carts of devices. Inconsistent access was the source of major frustration and caused an enormous disconnect between professional development and implementation.

Providing dedicated carts of devices could only be productive if teachers were given the professional development and networking support they needed. Teachers could receive up to $1000 in stipends for attending a one-day Saturday kickoff workshop, two two-hour after-school follow-up workshops, and spending additional hours working on their Project LEAN In portal page, blog, and asynchronous cycle of inquiry work. All applicants had to agree to attend the January 31st kickoff as part of the application process. By virtue of being in the first cohort, they do not just pilot 1:1 devices, they are teacher leaders at their sites. The first cohort mentors the second cohort, and so forth.

Just as we encourage collaboration and peer teaching among students, teachers will be collaborating and peer teaching themselves within their cohorts. In addition to vertical mentoring of one cohort to the next, there will be lateral mentoring within cohorts. The cycle of inquiry was the vehicle to clarify teaching and learning outcomes, and part of the kickoff training involved forming networks of critical friends that offered enough similarity to inspire cross-pollination and associational thinking.

One-Day Kickoff Workshop

The kickoff workshop was critical to building a cohesive cohort of teachers who would support each other and position their cycle of inquiry collaboratively. Applications ran the gamut from not fully thought out to too broad, but all had potential. Teachers also needed to know how their carts and devices functioned in the district's network before launching so they could comfortably manage their dedicated carts. They were also made aware of the assigned IT technician and CMS they could contact to increase their comfort level.

Each teacher was asked to bring the fully charged teacher toolkits they received at a summer or fall tech academy. (Four out of the five teachers who had not attended an academy attended an intensive full-day workshop to gain experience with Google apps and receive a toolkit.) There were eight sessions to expose teachers to topics critical to their independent survival. Each participant was given an individualized agenda so they knew the location and sequence of their sessions.

We started together for the welcome, overview, and introductions. Each teacher attended three 15-minute sessions, each regarding an aspect of their hardware, with five-minute passing periods between sessions. There were four 25-minute software/app sessions, one of which helped them start their Project LEAN In website using the project's Google Site template. Most of the afternoon was spent launching the cycle of inquiry work. Teachers were divided roughly into two groups (English Language Arts and Applied Arts) so they could hear about each other's projects. They subdivided into groups of 5–10 teachers to form networks of critical friends, and completed the project description they received in the Google Classroom session. We used Doodle to calendar the two follow-up workshops for both the ELA and applied arts groups.

Follow-Up Workshops

Attending two two-hour follow-up workshops was part of the professional development package. The first hour would be hands-on tech learning and the second was devoted to cycle of inquiry work so subgroups could give each other feedback and individuals could reflect on the changes they wanted to make to improve their projects. For instance, we deployed Office 365 E1 licenses for Office Online and Pro+ licenses to students and staff in time for the first follow-up workshop. Teachers brought their devices to examine the new productivity tools and OneNote as a lesson organizer.

The group really came alive, though, as they briefly shared the best thing that happened for them since the kickoff workshop as a result of Project LEAN In. The group broke into their small groups to exchange feedback on their cycle of inquiry. Many teachers needed clarification about metrics, or evidence they can cite to measure the impact of tech integration. We collectively viewed several teacher blogs and marveled at the variety of posts. There was an inspiring mix of how-tos, student work, and reflection that encouraged late bloggers to start writing and sparked new ideas for student projects.

Asynchronous Work

The rest of the stipend compensated teachers for asynchronous project work. Teachers are expected to continue collaborating asynchronously and by commenting on each other's blogs. They were asked to communicate with their cohort and other teachers in the district through blog posts and informal discussions in their professional learning communities. They were encouraged to lean in by being creative and stimulating creativity in their own way. They served as critical friends and pushed to be critical thinkers.

Onsite Coaching

Part of the Promise of Technology was to integrate technology in all professional development; TSAs who can offer mini-workshops as part of faculty or grade level meetings have been well-received in the past. In addition to centralized workshops that are open to all teachers in the district, teachers can tap into onsite coaching. The duties of the teacher on special assignment (TSA) for tech integration are evolving to meet the changing needs of teachers and the district. The goal is to have one onsite TSA for Technology Integration for Elementary and Secondary grades.

TSA by Committee

It has been extremely difficult to find teachers who are willing to leave their classrooms to be a Teacher on Special Assignment (TSA) full time. Then I got the notion to fill the need by inviting superstar teachers to form a team to perform this vital role by committee. (They're not really a committee, but I modified the phrase "Closer by Committee" from baseball, where the manager mixes and matches closing pitchers to the weakness of the opponent for that night.)

We used a Google Doc to lay out the themes for the trimesters and possible workshops they could lead. I invited them by email with the addresses in the BCC to protect their identities. We had a proposal meeting to explain what our goals were and to brainstorm. It is a tremendous learning opportunity for these teachers to cross-pollinate their ideas and work with tech-savvy teachers like themselves.

These teachers will be paid for their preparation time. A teacher from a private school was also invited to join the group to increase availability.

Mini-Conferences

Mini-conferences on district inservice days are another invigorating, engaging professional development option. The idea is to offer concurrent workshops so teachers can choose workshops that may or may not be planned to follow themes. A lot of pre-planning is involved, but the increased buy-in and engagement makes it worthwhile. Conferences can take place over the course of two days, or two half-day workshops on an inservice day.

One-Day Mini-Conference

Four teachers and I were so inspired while attending the CUE National Conference in Palm Springs in May 2015 that we came up with a new one-day mini-conference we called FEAST (Fun Engaging Accessible Summer Tech). Teachers and administrators were invited to get "cookin' with tech" by attending courses presented by teachers Brian Ortiz, Mickie Shannon, Alexis Meron, Recep Iscan, and myself in the following mini-conference:

- Sampler: getting a 10-minute taste of all five courses

- First course: a two-hour hands-on, make-it take-it session on a choice of:

  - Forms for Thought

  - Extravaganza of Infographs

  - All You Can Eat Apps

  - Slicin' and Dicin' with Slides

  - Toss-Up of Google Classroom and OneNote Class

- Second Course or Second Servings after lunch

- Sweet Ending with Cookies and Closing

Having fun, working hard, sharing good recipes, and customizing to taste were the order of the day.

Two-Day Mini-Conference (Keynote, Plus Five Sessions)

Five top tips when planning a two-day conference for your district (or what to ask for as a teacher):

1. Have teachers pre-register for sessions so all sessions are well-attended.

2. If possible, each teacher should bring their own laptop or device so every room is a potential venue.

3. Offer strands of sequential workshops. (For example: Google Sites Basics, Google Sites Intermediate, Google Sites Finishing Touches, Open Lab)

4. Offer an open lab with a coach so teachers can focus on their project instead of feeling overwhelmed with new material.

5. Make sure each presenting teacher has a chance to attend workshops too.

Half-Day Inservice

Giving teachers a choice on an inservice day takes the sting out of mandatory training. Top three tips:

1. Pair presentations so there is a choice of times or content in two parts or levels. For example: GAFE Basics on Chromebooks, Google Forms; Guided Reading, Guided Reading (Encore).

2. Split the day: choice of workshops in the morning; work at sites in the afternoon.

3. Have teachers pre-register for sessions.

The combinations of professional learning opportunities are limitless. Haphazard, serendipitous learning has its merits because it is unimposing and easy to fall into. Planned paths that are a mix of face-to-face workshops, online tutorials, and higher education programs ensure a constant upward spiral of learning. The cliché "The only constant is change" is so apropos in technology—a lifelong learner's dream.

Teacher Leadership

The underlying purpose of all of this professional development is to build capacity and teacher leadership. The most meaningful and applicable tech integration comes from fellow teachers. The job of district leadership is to nurture teacher leadership.

The Technology Academies provided a foundation of technology skills, toolkits, and immersion in a 1:1 device-learner environment. Project LEAN In made it easy for teachers to step forward to pioneer and share their process, professional growth, and passion. The work of this network of teachers created momentum and excitement for Cohort 2, as 68 teachers submitted high-quality applications. There is anticipation for Cohort 3, 4, and 5, provided funding can be found. Implementation based on interest and commitment, not numbers, has brought out our teacher leaders. It is their actions, not position, that makes them leaders.

Summary

What   Professional learning in the Innovation Age needs to mirror what our students need to learn. Professional development needs to be about and model collaboration, communication, creativity, and critical thinking in a 1:1 blended learning environment.

So What   Teachers need a strategic approach to professional development to take full advantage of opportunities in the fast-changing ed tech landscape.

Now What   Instead of taking a "divide and conquer" approach to learning teachers should take a collaborative, team approach so they can immediately integrate new learning into lessons and long term change.

Up Next...

Ending Digital Isolation

Equity demands that no student or teacher is isolated digitally or physically from the resources they need.

CHAPTER **10**

Ending
Digital Isolation

Isolation is a dream killer.

— Barbara Sher, author and career counselor

One-to-one, learner-to-device ratio has to be the Innovation Age standard for student access. Without consistent access, technology is not a seamless, fully integrated part of learning. Wireless access was born because people could not have consistent access to the Internet by taking turns plugging their computer into available drops. How is it that we continue to see students waiting for their turn to go to the computer lab, or finding that devices are already checked out for use?

In order to fully infuse technology into the curriculum, as called for by Common Core standards, teachers must find a way to get continuous access to technology for their students. Technology has to become an invisible part of the learning environment.

The National Educational Technology Plan *Transforming American Education: Learning Powered by Technology* (Office of Educational Technology, 2011) describes continuous access to learning as "always-on." Executive Summary item 1.3 states:

> The always-on nature of the Internet and mobile access devices provides our education system with the opportunity to create learning experiences that are available anytime and anywhere. When combined with design principles for personalized learning and Universal Design for Learning, these experiences also can be accessed by learners who have been marginalized in many educational settings: students from low-income communities and minorities, English language learners, students with disabilities, students who are gifted and talented, students from diverse cultures and linguistic backgrounds, and students in rural areas.

The plan recommends at least a 1:1 device to student and educator in Section 4.2:

> Ensure that every student and educator has at least one Internet access device and appropriate software and resources for research, communication, multimedia content creation, and collaboration for use in and out of school. Only with 24/7 access to the internet via devices and tech-based software and resources can we achieve the kind of engagement, student-centered learning, and assessments that can improve learning in the ways this plan proposes. The form of these devices, software, and resources may not be standardized and will evolve over time. In addition, these devices may be owned by the student or family, owned by the school, or some combination of the two. The use of devices owned by students will require advances in network filtering and improved support systems.

State and local public education institutions must ensure equitable access to learning experiences for all students and especially students in underserved populations—low-income and minority students, and students with disabilities.

Equity

Equity has been a challenge for every district that I have worked in and with for decades now. Administrators in my current district have met every month for seven years to find solutions and keep the issue front and center. We strive to examine everything through an equity lens. We were talking about the stereotypical "lost boy" who sits on the timeout bench at too many of our elementary sites. This separation was imposed inside of classrooms too—the seat right up front next to the board, corner seats in the back of the room, or in a separate "timeout" space. This child is not only cut off from his peers, but he has lost access to the curriculum and learning.

It made me think about how damaging isolation is. The worst offenders in prison are isolated and given solitary confinement. Physical isolation, whether it is self-imposed or imposed by others, hurts in so many ways.

Then I thought about how isolated I feel when I don't have my smart phone or computer to keep me connected to the world. Being disconnected is not just inconvenient for me—I cannot do my job, I feel unsafe, and I feel isolated. It dawned on me that when students in the Innovation Age lack access, no matter what the reason, they are digitally isolated. None of my schools have achieved the 1:1 device to learner ratio that is recommended in the National Education Technology Plan, so there are long periods when students are digitally isolated. It's not just a matter of providing devices, wireless access, or resources; some of our teachers choose not to integrate technology in their classrooms because they are not comfortable using computers, Chromebooks, tablets, or online resources.

Equity in the Innovation Age requires that we end digital isolation. Our students cannot afford to continue to learn in the classrooms their teachers grew up in because the world has changed. There was no technology in the classroom when I grew up and I did just fine, but no one else in my generation had technology in his or her classroom. By refusing to infuse technology today, a teacher is imposing digital isolation upon their students, much like the student who is on the bench or in "timeout." When will this child recover from this isolation?

Consistent Student Access at School

To frame it in the positive, every student and teacher should have consistent access to devices and the internet. The National Education Technology Plan calls for "always-on" learning, 24/7 access to the internet via devices for every student and teacher to enable them to do research, collaborate, communicate, and create multimedia content, in and out of school. The multimillion-dollar question is: how do we achieve this?

In my district, this means starting with increasing the number of devices for students so every student has access to an internet-connected device while they are in school. (The district standard is that every teacher be supplied with a desktop computer and monitor in their classroom.) The key initiatives for this goal are:

- Improving wireless access
- Supporting site-based purchases of devices
- Providing district-based support for lead teachers
- Pursuing bond money to support technology implementation

Wireless Access

We completed a wireless network upgrade in the summer of 2014 to make it possible for every student and teacher in every classroom to be on the internet simultaneously. Prior to the upgrade, wireless was concentrated near testing venues, and the access points started to drop users when 20 or so of them were logged on. The issue was not bandwidth, as most teachers thought, because we were consistently at around 10% of bandwidth. Yes, 90% of what we paid for was not being used. AND you needed new access points? The new "smart" wireless access points we installed made a huge difference. The old ones could only accommodate 25 users before they started dropping off. We were able to run YouTube on 76 Chromebooks off one isolated wireless access point on the initial test. After making a few adjustments, we were able to run YouTube videos on 100 Chromebooks simultaneously before we ran out of devices for the test. With the new configuration, we were able to replace the 600 wireless access points in the district with 440 new ones.

It took some time before teachers trusted wireless access enough to integrate mobile devices into their lessons. Six months after upgrading the wireless network, overall usage tripled to an average of 30% of bandwidth. The wireless upgrade may not account for all the increase, but it most certainly contributed to greater use of technology.

Site-based Purchases

2014–2015 was the last year of local bond funding for the classrooms in our district. Half of Measure O provides funding for classroom technology based on decisions made by site technology committees. The money could not be spent on consumable items. As a newbie director, I tried two things that had a positive impact on site-based purchases.

I tried to get myself invited to as many schools as possible to do site-based visioning meetings so that principals and tech committee members did not bear the full responsibility of making purchases. Visioning meetings consisted of the "We Have a Dream" presentation to explain the district vision for technology integration and the four promises I mentioned previously in Chapter 8. This made the tech leaders look like heroes, as well they should, for seeking collaborative decision-making, broad-based input, and buy-in up front. I do not think it was a coincidence that the sites that invited me to do a visioning meeting had the highest rate of participation in the Summer Technology Academies.

The other thing that worked well was to partner with principals to focus on purchasing devices for student use. First of all, I was very transparent about equitably allocating Measure O funds to sites based on unduplicated student counts while holding harmless sites that would have experienced a decrease in their funding. (Unduplicated student count is new to California. Students used to be counted in each program, but now they are counted once whether they are homeless or in foster care, English language learners, receiving Special Education services, or in the free or reduced-priced lunch programs. In 2014–15 our unduplicated student count was at 73%.) I also made funds available as early as Business Services would allow so devices could be ready at the start of the school year. Our compromise was that sites could spend all of the new year's allocation and dip into the previous year's carryover once the fiscal year was closed out.

School sites have other funds available to them for tech purchases. Some sites have used Common Core funds and others have used categorical monies. There has been talk about floating another bond measure, but it will take a while before those monies would be available to schools.

District-based 1:1 Device Initiative – Project LEAN In

We adapted our neighbor's idea for providing 1:1 devices to learners in classrooms as one of our Local Control Accountability Plan (LCAP) initiatives. Technology for student use came up as a priority in almost every one of the 43-plus community input meetings, so we used some one-time monies to fund Project LEAN In (LEAN stands for Learning Environments that increase Access and target Needs. Teachers can be "In" to inspire, intrigue, involve, instruct, invite, and so forth. (As long as they are in.) Our neighbor San Leandro Unified School District turned 75 classrooms in the district into "21st-century classrooms" through their "Instructional Innovators" program, which provided equipment and professional development to successful teachers who applied to the program.

In 2014–15, the San Lorenzo Unified School District provided each of the 37 teachers in Cohort 1 of Project LEAN In with a dedicated cart of mobile devices to bring their classes to a 1:1 student to device ratio. Teachers participated in the mandatory kickoff workshop, and could receive up to $1,000 in stipends based on participation in workshops, working on their blogs, and working on their tech-infusion-related cycle of inquiry projects. Although the district had initially hoped to fund 100 classrooms in 2014–15, competing priorities and the state budget made it necessary to cut the program. In hindsight, 100 teachers in a single cohort would have been too much for us to manage effectively.

There are just under 600 teachers in the district so funding Cohort 2 was a high priority. The district encumbered the Microsoft Settlement money to fund another 40 teachers for the 2015–16 school year. By securing funding the prior spring, applications were made available in April, the kickoff occurred the week before school started, and teachers started the year with carts in their classrooms. We advocated for funding for Cohort 3 (2016–17) in the 2015–16 budget so teachers would start the year with devices, unlike Cohort 1, which did not receive its dedicated carts until February 2014.

I am steering away from two popular programs because of unique local conditions.

- **BYOD.** I am avoiding Bring Your Own Device (BYOD) because we had students hijacked for their devices (which are worth more than lunch money) and because the size of the devices makes it difficult for students to comfortably create substantial documents, produce multimedia projects, or do deep research.

- **Flipped Classroom.** Until more students and their families can afford devices and internet connectivity, we are up against an equity issue. It is on my radar to revisit this decision after we have greater access to devices for students at school and more continuous integration of technology, and can provide more support for 1:1 access at home.

1:1 At School and At Home

Establishing a culture of 1:1 device to learner means that 24/7 access is available, at home as well as at school. It means that teachers are immersed in a culture of 1:1 mobile devices in their professional learning so they are not only comfortable using technology, but are dependent on it to be effective and efficient.

Once the excitement about using technology gives way to excitement about the content, the value of 1:1 access will be realized.

As that transformation takes place we plan to establish partnerships with nonprofits such as http://everyoneon.com to provide access to devices and the internet at home. We plan to extend resources such as Microsoft Office 365 district-wide to provide options in addition to Google Apps.

When we end digital isolation for all learners, we keep dreams alive.

Summary

What	Equity in the Innovation Age requires that we end digital isolation. Any child who lacks access to technology is cut off from the world and receives a substandard education.
So What	Teachers need to be aware of the many programs they can pursue, so they and their district partners can ensure that their students have consistent access to technology.
Now What	Achieve 1:1 device to learner access at school and at home to end digital isolation.

Up Next...

Get ready to fully prepare all students to thrive in the Innovation Age.

APPENDIX A
Summary and Findings of Dissertation Study

This summary of the dissertation study *Learning through Student-Authored Interactive Media: A Mixed Methods Exploration* (Sakai-Miller, 2009) describes the study and the measures that were used to gauge its success.

Successful Study

The study examined two key issues in education reform: the need to improve student achievement in science and information; and information communication technology (ICT) skills. Instead of isolating the issues, the study explored an integrated solution that applied the constructivist approach to help students learn about biology concepts while building "eModules." The eModules the students constructed were essentially interactive presentations that combined informational summaries, pictures, animations, and self-correcting, self-scoring quizzes. The unit of study on mitosis, the cell cycle, and cancer was completed in two weeks.

The study's premise: the instructional strategy of student-authored interactive media would enhance learning of science content and foster proficiency in ICT skills. Four research questions drove the study:

1. What was the extent of learning, as determined by comparison of the pre- and posttests, for students who author eModules?

2. What do students experience as they proceed through the following steps: a) creating concept maps to organize science content, b) designing slides to integrate biology content and generate quiz questions, c) developing eModules to make their presentations self-scoring and interactive, and d) analyzing their progress?

3. What obstacles did students confront and document in their journals or exit surveys during the process of authoring eModules?

4. What did the teachers experience providing tech support and other instructional needs to help students to author eModules?

The study took place at a comprehensive public high school in a suburban corner of the Central Valley of Northern California. Students in Grades 11–12 participated in the first of the two-year advanced biology courses in the International Baccalaureate (IB) program. Students were not pre-screened or tracked into the program. Any student at the school could enroll in Advanced Biology as long as they had passed biology and chemistry.

To limit the "teacher variable" and keep the instruction and classroom resources as consistent as possible, the study was limited to students in two sections of IB Advanced Biology taught by the same teacher. Of the 57 students enrolled in the two classes, 89% (51 students) submitted assent (student) and consent (parental) forms. Qualitative data were taken from the 51 student journals and exit surveys, although all 57 students working in groups of two or three completed their eModules.

Evidence of Standards-Based Learning

Although the potential number of pre- and posttest scores we could compare was 51, due to absence only 45 11th and 12th graders took the teacher-designed 74-pt multiple choice and short essay unit exam at the beginning and end of the two-week unit. Test questions written by the participating teacher were similar to those used in previous years and were consistent with assessment and grading standards established by the International Baccalaureate programs. The participating teacher used the rubric marking system specified in the IB Biology program to score both tests to ensure consistency in assessing the short essay questions.

Let's compare the scores for all students in Figure A.1. The pretest scores are in gray, and the improvement between pre- and posttest scores are in black, so the total posttest score is the combined gray and black bar. The scores are arranged in ascending order based on each student's pretest score.

This chart startled a board member who had earlier asked why I was so passionate about educational technology. All 45 students showed improvement. The implications for a Program Improvement district like ours were huge!

Before you look at the scores, I want to acknowledge inherent limitations to studies that compare pre- and posttest scores. Students who take the posttest were exposed to the same questions on the pretest, so they should do better the second time. Students do not have much incentive to do well on a pretest; their initial scores may not accurately reflect their knowledge. There is also the question of the Hawthorne effect—how much of the improvement in learning can be attributed to students being aware they are participating in a study. The nature of the study is exploratory, not experimental, and it was not possible or realistic to randomize participation to minimize this effect. While the Hawthorne effect may account for some increase, the 1229% average change in scores for students who earned less than 10% on the pretest cannot be solely attributed to the effect alone.

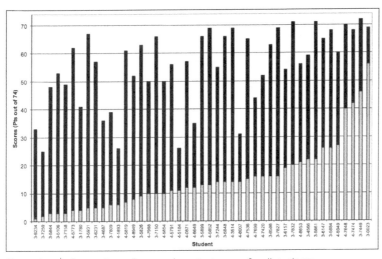

Figure A.1 | Comparison of pre- and posttest scores for all students

All Students

Improvement for individual students was calculated by finding the difference (posttest score minus pretest score) and represented as a percentage (difference divided by posttest score).

Here are some items from analyzing data for all students in the study:

- The average improvement for students in the study was 547%

- Student improvement ranged from a minimum of 23% to a maximum of 3200%

- The lowest pretest score was one point (1%) and the highest, 56 points (75%), for a mean score of 15 points (20%)

- The lowest posttest score was 25 points (34%) and the highest, 72 points (97%), for a mean score of 55.5 points (75%)

- The student who made the least improvement (23%) had the top pre-test score and went from 75% to 93% on the test

- The student who made the most improvement (3200%) had the lowest pre-test score and went from 1% to 40% on the test

Students with Low Initial Scores

Students with low initial scores (10% or less on the pretest) showed the most improvement, which is significant to people charged with closing the achievement gap (Figure A.2). Three students with low initial scores actually improved so much that they were also in the "big gainers" group (students who scored 20% or less on the pretest and 80% or above on the posttest).

Here are some interesting results for students with low initial scores:

- The mean pretest score was four (6%)

- The average improvement was 1229%, as compared to 547% for all students

- Despite their greater gains, the mean posttest score of 46 (62%) was 13% lower than the mean posttest score of 55 (75%) for all students

- While 63% of the student sample was female, 92% of students with low initial scores were female

- Twelfth graders comprised 20% of the student sample, but 39% of the students with low initial scores.

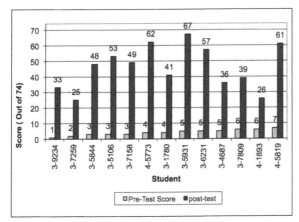

Figure A.2 | Comparison of pre- and posttest scores for students with low initial scores.

Big Gainers

When you think of the big gainers in the study, think 20-20-80; 20% of the students scored 20% or less on the pretest and improved 80% or more on the posttest.

Here is a summary of the data for big gainers:

- Three of the 10 big gainers had pretest scores below 10%

- The mean pretest score was 14%; the mean posttest score was 88%

- The big gainers experienced a 656% mean improvement, as compared to 547% for all students

- All big gainers were 11th graders, although they comprised 80% of all students

- 80% of big gainers were female, although they comprised 64% of all students

Students with High Initial Scores

The smallest sub-group was students with high initial scores (over 50%). All four students scored over 90% on the posttest, which suggests that the instructional strategy was not detrimental to high-achieving students. The mean improvement for students with high initial scores was 54% as compared to 547% for all students, but with initial scores of 50% or better, it would not be possible to improve by more than 100% (Table A.1). Although the sample size is too small to draw conclusions about students with high initial scores, isn't it interesting that all of them were 11th graders and evenly split between male and female.

Table A.1 | Scores for High Initial Scores Subgroup

Student	Gender	Grade	Pretest Scores		Posttest Scores		Improvement
			Pts out of 74	%	Pts out of 74	%	%
4-7648	F	11	40	54%	70	95%	75%
4-7474	M	11	42	57%	68	92%	62%
3-7449	M	11	46	62%	72	97%	57%
3-0023	F	11	56	76%	69	93%	23%
		Min	40	54%	68	92%	23%
		Max	56	76%	72	97%	75%
		Mean	46	62%	69.75	94%	54%
		Std Dev	7.12	10%	1.71	2%	22%

APPENDIX B
References

Ainsworth, L. (2011). *Rigorous curriculum design: How to create curricular units of study that align standards, instruction, and assessment.* Englewood, CO: Lead+Learn Press.

Aldrich, C. (2005). *Learning by doing: The essential guide to simulations, computer games, and pedagogy in e-learning and other educational experiences.* San Francisco, CA: Pfeiffer.

Allery, L. A. (2004). Educational games and structured experiences. *Medical Teacher, 26*(6), 504-505.

Bannan-Ritland, B. (2002). Computer-mediated communication, elearning, and interactivity. *Quarterly Review of Distance Education 3*(2), 161-179.

Barab, S., Thomas, M., Dodge, T., Carteaux, R., & Tuzun, H. (2005). Making learning fun: Quest Atlantis, a game without guns. *Educational Technology Research & Development,* volume, 86-107.

Bassoppo-Moyo, T. (2006). Evaluating elearning: A front-end, process and post hoc approach. *International Journal of Instructional Media, 33*(1), 7-22.

Beck, J. C., & Wade, M. (2004) *Got game: How the gamer generation is reshaping business forever.* Cambridge, MA: Harvard Business School Press.

Brigham Young University (2006). Expected learning outcomes. Retrieved October 14, 2014, from https://learningoutcomes.byu.edu.

Brown, K. (2005). Technology: Building interaction. *Tech Trends, 49*(5), 36-38.

Bull, G., Thompson, A., Searson, M., Garofalo, J., Park, J., Young, C., et al. (2008). Connecting informal and formal learning experiences in the age of participatory media. *Contemporary Issues in Technology and Teacher Education, 8*(2),100-107.

Cambourne, B. (2002). The conditions of learning: Is learning natural? *The Reading Teacher, 55*(8), 758-762.

Carstens, A. & Beck, J. (2005). Get ready for the gamer generation. *Tech Trends: Linking Research & Practice to Improve Learning, 49*(3), 22-25.

Cassarino, C. (2003). Instructional design principles for an elearning environment. *Quarterly Review of Distance Education, 4*(4), 455-461.

Critical Thinking – Dictionary.com. Retrieved October 4, 2014, from http://dictionary.reference.com/browse/critical+thinking

Department of Education, 2011. STEM - U.S. Department of Education. Retrieved October 11, 2014, from https://www2.ed.gov/about/overview/budget/budget12/crosscuttingissues/stemed.pdf.

DeKanter, N. (2005). Gaming redefines interactivity for learning. *Tech Trends: Linking Research & Practice to Improve Learning, 49*(3), 26-31.

Dori, Y. J., & Belcher, J. (2005). Learning electromagnetism with visualizations and active learning. *Visualization in Science Education,* 187-216.

Dyer, J., Gregerson, H. & Christensen, C. M. (2011). *Innovator's DNA, Mastering the five skills of disruptive innovators.* Cambridge, MA: Harvard Business School Press.

Educational Testing Service. (2006). Standards for quality and fairness. Princeton, NJ

Edwards, C. J., Carr, S., & Siegel, W. (2006). Influences of experiences and training on effective teaching practices to meet the needs of diverse learners in schools. *Education, 126*(3), 580-592.

Evans, C. & Sabry, K. (2003). Evaluations of the interactivity of web-based learning systems: Principles and process. *Innovations in Education and Teaching International, 40*(1), 89-99.

Gee, J. P. (2003). *What video games have to teach us about learning and literacy.* New York: Palgrave Macmillan.

Gee, J. P. (2005). Good video games and good learning. *Phi Kappa Phi Forum, 85*(2), 33-37.

Gelb, M. J. (2000). *How to think like Leonardo da Vinci.* New York, NY: Dell Publishing.

Hattori, R. A., & J. Wycoff. (2004). *Innovation Training*. Alexandria, VA: ASTD Press.

Hirumi, A. (2002). A framework for analyzing, designing, and sequencing planned elearning interactions. *Quarterly Review of Distance Education, 3*(2), 141-160.

Horn, M. B., & Staker, H. (2011). The rise of K-12 blended learning. Innosight Institute.

Innovation—Merriam-Webster. Retrieved October 11, 2014, from www.merriam-webster.com/dictionary/innovation.

International Society for Technology Education (2008). National educational technology standards for teachers. Eugene, OR: *International Society for Technology In Education*.

Jana, R. (2005). The many ways to make a game. *Business Week Online*. Retrieved 12/27/2007 from www.businessweek.com/innvate/content/nov2005/id20051107_181961.htm.

Jonassen, D. H. (2003). Using cognitive tools to represent problems. *Journal of Research on Technology in Education, 35*(3), 362-381.

Jonassen, D. H. (2006). A constructivist's perspective on functional contextualism. *Educational Technology Research & Development, 54*(1), 43-47.

Jonassen, D. H., Carr, C., & Yueh, H. P. (1998). Computers as mindtools for engaging learners in critical thinking. *Tech Trends, 43*(2), 24-32.

Juniu, S. (2006). Use of technology for constructivist learning in a performance assessment class. *Measurement in Physical Education and Exercise Science, 10*(1), 67-79.

Kaiser Family Foundation, (2005). *Generation m: Kaiser Family Foundation*.

Kelley, David. (2013). IDEO on 60 Minutes and CBS This Morning | IDEO. Retrieved April 7, 2015, from http://www.ideo.com/60minutes/.

Kelley, T. & and Kelley, D., (2013). *Creative confidence: Unleashing the creative potential within us all*. New York: Crown Business.

Klopfer, E. & Yoon, S. (2005). Developing games and simulations for today and tomorrow's tech savvy youth. *Tech Trends: Linking Research & Practice to Improve Learning, 49*(3), 33-41.

Lierman, B. (1994). How to develop a training simulation. *Training & Development, 48*(2), 50-53.

Luján-Mora, S., & de Juana-Espinosa, S. (2007). The use of weblogs in higher education: Benefits and barriers. *Proceedings of the International Technology, Education and Development Conference* (INTED 2007).

Lyle, S. (2000). Narrative understanding: Developing a theoretical context for understanding how children make meaning in classroom settings. *Journal of Curriculum Studies, 32*(1), 45-66.

Malone, T. W. (1980). What makes things fun to learn? Heuristics for designing instructional computer games. *I SIGSMALL '80: Proceeding of the 3 ACM SIGSMALL symposium and the first SIGPC symposium on small systems,* 162-169. New York: ACM Press.

Mangis, C. A. (August 5, 2005). Play with a purpose. *PC Magazine, 24*(13), 20.

McLester, J.(2005). Game plan: Part 2, student gamecraft. *Technology & Learning, 26*(4), 20-24.

Medina, J. (2008). *Brain rules: 12 principles for surviving and thriving at work. home, and school.* Seattle, WA: Pear Press.

Michalko, M. (2006). *Thinkertoys: A handbook of creative-thinking techniques.* Berkeley, CA: Ten Speed Press.

Modi, T. (2011). *Living in the innovation age: Five principles for prospering in the new era.* Springfield, VA: TekNirvana.

Montessori, Maria. (n.d.). BrainyQuote.com. Retrieved April 6, 2015, from www.brainyquote.com/quotes/quotes/m/mariamonte403452.htm.

Moran, M., Seaman, J., & Tinti-Kane, H. (2011). *Teaching, learning, and sharing: How today's higher education faculty use social media.* Pearson Learning Solutions.

Moreno, R., & Mayer, R. E. (2005). Role of guidance, reflection, and interactivity in an agent-based multimedia game. *Journal of Educational Psychology, 97*(1), 117-128.

Morphew, V. (2012). A constructivist approach to the national educational technology standards for teachers. International Society for Technology in Education.

National Academy of Sciences, (1999). *Being fluent with information technology,* Washington, DC: National Academy Press.

NETP (2011). Transforming american education: learning powered by technology. Retrieved August 31, 2012, from https://www.ed.gov/sites/default/files/netp2010.pdf.

Obama, Barack, 2011. A strategy for American innovation: Securing our economic ... Retrieved April 7, 2015, from https://www.whitehouse.gov/innovation/strategy.

Ohl, T. M. (2001). An interaction-centric learning model. *Journal of Educational Multimedia and Hypermedia, 10*(4), 311-332.

OnInnovation : Visionaries thinking out loud™ - powered by ... Retrieved April 7, 2015, from http://www.oninnovation.com.

Papert, S. (1993). *The children's machine: Rethinking school in the age of the computer.* New York: BasicBooks.

Parker, K., & Chao, J. (2007). Wiki as a teaching tool. *Interdisciplinary Journal of e-learning and Learning Objects, 3*(1), 57-72.

Pew Internet, 2011.

Prensky, M. (2006). *Don't bother me mom——I'm learning!* St. Paul, MN: Paragon House.

Quinn, C. N. (2005). *Engaging learning: Designing e-learning simulation games.* San Francisco, CA: Pfeiffer.

Raine, L., Purcell, K., & Smith, A, (2011). The Social Side of the Internet. Pew Research Center. Retrieved October 4, 2014, from www.pewinternet.org/2011/01/18/the-social-side-of-the-internet/.

Robertson, J., & Good, J. (2005). Children's narrative development through computer game authoring, *Tech Trends, 49*(5), 43-59.

Sakai-Miller, S. (2009). *Learning through student-authored interactive media: A mixed methods exploration.*

Salen, K., & Zimmerman, E. (2004). *Rules of play: Game design fundamentals.* Cambridge, MA: The MIT Press.

Seelig, T. (2012). in Genius: *A Crash Course on Creativity.* New York: HarperCollins.

Simpson, E. S. (2005). What teachers need to know about the video game generation. *TechTrends: Linking Research & Practice to Improve Learning, 49*(5), 17-22.

6 Free Tools to Easily Cite Resources for Students and ... Retrieved April 7, 2015, from www.educatorstechnology.com/2012/04/6-free-tools-to-easily-cite-resources.html.

Squire, K., Giovanetto, L., Devane, B., & Durga, S. (2005). From users to designers: Building a self-organizing game-based learning environment. *TechTrends, 49*(5), 34-42.

Tapscott, Don, (2013). "The Spirit of Collaboration Is Touching All of Our Lives." Speech to Trent University graduating class. Retrieved April 6, 2015, from http://www.huffingtonpost.com/don-tapscott/the-spirit-of-collaborati_b_3421400.html.

Voight, Joan, (2014). Which big brands are courting the maker movement, and ... Retrieved April 7, 2015, from www.adweek.com/news/advertising-branding/which-big-brands-are-courting-maker-movement-and-why-156315.

Vygotsky, L. S. (1978). *Mind in society: The development of higher psychological processes.* Cambridge, MA: Harvard University Press.

Wagner, T., 2012. *Creating innovators: The making of young people who will change the world.* New York: Scribner.

Wang, Y. M. (2006). Technology projects as a vehicle to empower students. *Educational Media International, 43*(4), 315-330.

Watson, J. (2008). Blended learning: The convergence of online and face-to-face education. iNACOL.

Watson, J., Murin, A., Vashaw, L., Gemin, B., & Rapp, C. (2011). Keeping pace with K–12 online learning: An annual review of policy and practice, 2011. Evergreen Education Group.

Wenger, E. (1998). *Communities of practice: Learning, meaning, and identity.* Cambridge, MA: Harvard Business School Press.

Westervelt, 2014. College Applicants Sweat The SATs. Perhaps They Shouldn ... Retrieved April 7, 2015, from www.npr.org/2014/02/18/277059528/ college-applicants-sweat-the-sats-perhaps-they-shouldn-t.

Wiliam, D. (2011). *Embedded formative assessment.* Bloomington, IN: Solution Tree Press.

Wolpert-Gawron, H. (2014). Supporting the teacher maker movement | *Edutopia.* Retrieved April 7, 2015, from www.edutopia.org/blog/ supporting-teacher-maker-movement-heather-wolpert-gawron.

Zhao, Y. (2011). *World class learners: Educating creative and entrepreneurial students.* Thousand Oaks, CA: Corwin Press, and SAGE Publications.

Zhu, E. & Baylens, D. M. (2005). From learning community to community learning: Pedagogy, technology and interactivity. *Educational Media International,* 42(3), 251-268.

Index